Ghosts of ALASKA

Stories & Legends from the Last Frontier

Schiffer Publishing Ltd

Jody Ellis-Knapp

880 Lower Valley Road, Atglen, Pennsylvania 19310

Schiffer Books are available at special discounts for bulk purchases for sales promotions or premiums. Special editions, including personalized covers, corporate imprints, and excerpts can be created in large quantities for special needs. For more information contact the publisher:

Published by Schiffer Publishing Ltd.
4880 Lower Valley Road
Atglen, PA 19310
Phone: (610) 593-1777; Fax: (610) 593-2002
E-mail: Info@schifferbooks.com

For the largest selection of fine reference books on this and related subjects,
please visit our web site at: **www.schifferbooks.com**
We are always looking for people to write books on new and related subjects.
If you have an idea for a book please contact us at the above address.

This book may be purchased from the publisher.
Include $5.00 for shipping.
Please try your bookstore first.
You may write for a free catalog.

In Europe, Schiffer books are distributed by
Bushwood Books
6 Marksbury Ave.
Kew Gardens
Surrey TW9 4JF England
Phone: 44 (0) 20 8392 8585; Fax: 44 (0) 20 8392 9876
E-mail: info@bushwoodbooks.co.uk
Website: www.bushwoodbooks.co.uk

Printed in the United States of America

Cover photo: Waterside Cross © Guy Sagi. Photo courtesy BigStockPhotos.com
Cruise Ship Anchored In Harbor © Steve Estvanik. Ship in Sunset © Daniil Kirillov.
Photos courtesy of BigStockPhotos.com.

Other Schiffer Books on Related Subjects
Alaskan Maritime, 0-7643-0035-0, $29.95
Supernatural Hawaii, 978-0-7643-3186-2, $16.99
Spirits and Death in Niagra, 978-0-7643-2695-4, $14.99

Copyright © 2009 by Jody Ellis-Knapp
Library of Congress Control Number: 2009922317

Designed by Mark David Bowyer
Type set in Scratch Board / NewsGoth BT

ISBN: 978-0-7643-3303-3
Printed in the United States of America

Contents

Introduction

Alaska is a relatively young state when compared to the rest of the United States. As one of the last territories to become a state and one of the furthest removed from the rest of the "Lower 48" – as we call the continental United States – our nickname of "The Last Frontier" is quite apt. Alaska has long been considered a place to go when one is running away from the world (hence our other nefarious nickname, "Home of America's Most Wanted") and the place where working hard really can bring wealth and success. Alaska today is much more urban than those frontier days, but we still enjoy endless vistas of untouched wilderness, a fairly low unemployment rate, and a smaller population overall.

Unfortunately, Alaska is also one of the most violent places in the country, especially when considering that small population. We have some of the highest percentages of rapes and domestic disturbance in the country, as well as having the dubious award of being the state with the highest level of alcoholism. Long cold winters can lead to cabin fever, which all contribute to sometimes bringing out the worst in people.

The history here is colorful and often brutal. Gold Rush fever took over in the 1800s and Alaska went from being a relatively untouched rough country to a mecca of tent cities and prospectors staking their claims. As often happens with the influx of sudden wealth – or just the promise of wealth – violence, anger, and despair went right alongside those gold nuggets that could make or break a man.

Add in some natural disasters, like the 1964 earthquake, oppression and violence against Alaska's native peoples, and the oil boom of the 1970s followed by the huge crash in the 1980s, the history of Alaska becomes a hotbed of intrigue, murder, mayhem, sorrow, and desperation—it's all here and is evident throughout our history.

It's been said that when a person dies violently or from unusual circumstances, their spirit remains behind in a perpetual state of conflict, so it's not surprising that despite the youth of the state as a whole, we still have our share of ghost stories. People murdered, committing suicide, having violent accidents, or just losing their way in the wilds of this country...they have somehow remained here to make their presence known to the living. Perhaps they want to send a message to their loved ones or could it be that they loved life too much to ever really leave it?

One of the things I love about Alaska is the connection that exists between the people here. No matter where you go or who you meet, if you've lived here a long time, it's almost a given that you'll run into someone you know, or will have friends in common with any random person you meet. I always joke that I live in the world's biggest small town because Alaska is just that.

Despite the fact that it's the largest state, despite the vast expanses of empty land between towns, or lack of road access in many areas, there always seems to be some kind of link between the people here. I found this to be true in my research, as every ghost story I heard seemed to be connected to another story. I would interview someone about a rumored haunting, and they would tell me stories of other places and incidents that they had heard about. Then when I followed up on that story, I would hear yet another story!

I am somewhat of an anomaly, in that I am a born and bred Alaskan of non-native heritage. My brothers and both of my children were also born here. A high percentage of the population of Alaska are "imports" from other states, drawn here by the oil fields and potential jobs, assigned here by the military, or brought here by an innate sense of adventure. My own grandparents had that sense of adventure. As a young couple with a child (my dad), they made their way from Texas to Alaska at the flip of a quarter. My grandfather used to tell the story of their decision to move here: "Well, I was an iron worker and a small plane pilot. I figured we could make a lot of money either in Alaska or Australia, so we flipped a coin—and Alaska it was!" Funny to think I might have grown up an Australian girl rather than an Alaskan girl!

I've spent many years traveling the world. I've seen places that are simply amazing, from the dramatic beauty of the desert, the California mountains, and the jungles of Mexico. I've ventured into the northern regions of Thailand, where we rode elephants from a small village, hopped on a raft in a slow moving river, and made our way downstream. I've seen Paris at night, been rained on amongst the green hills of Ireland, and watched the changing of the guard at Buckingham Palace. All of it has a unique splendor all its own and some places more beautiful than others, but all remarkable in their own way.

Yet no matter where I travel, inevitably that longing towards home begins after a few weeks. I miss waking up to the clear air of a still relatively unpolluted place. I miss the mountains always in my sight, a backdrop to everything I do. I miss going to the store and without a doubt seeing someone I know. I miss my friends, my family, all of it. Alaska is like no other. In all my travels, I have yet to find a place that compares. It really is like nowhere else on earth. And with all this magnificence, the ghost stories, legends, and people behind them are just a bit larger than life too.

I haven't decided yet if I am a believer or a skeptic. Even after hearing all the stories, writing them down, and talking endlessly to people all around the state, I'm just not sure if I believe in ghosts or that spirits haunt us. On the other hand, I've had some inexplicable experiences myself over the years, so it's hard to remain completely cynical in the face of evidence that almost proves that there is something to these stories. What that something is, I don't know. How many of these stories are true? Well, I don't know that either. So much of what I wrote was based on rumors and whispers and generational tales passed down from elder to child. And that is part of the beauty of the stories—you can be a believer or a skeptic and still find enjoyment in the telling of the tales themselves.

This book was created as a historical accounting of those ghost stories and haunted places. While there is a lot of true history included in the stories, this is a fictionalized book and is intended as entertainment, not as a way to prove or disprove the existence of ghosts in our world. The stories are just that—stories. Read with enjoyment, read with a light heart, and perhaps take away something from the stories—a grain of truth, a moment of revelation, or a thought that perhaps, just perhaps, there is more to our world than meets the eye.

Part One
Southcentral Alaska

HISTORIC
ANCHORAGE HOTEL
EST. 1916

CONSTRUCTED IN 1936, THIS BUILDING
REMAINS ON IT'S ORIGINAL SITE. IT
SURVIVED THE MARCH 27, 1964 EARTHQUAKE.
MAJOR RENOVATION WAS COMPLETED IN 1989.

The exterior of the Historic Anchorage Hotel, one of the oldest buildings in the city of Anchorage and one of the most haunted places in the state. *Photo by Jody Ellis-Knapp.*

Chapter One

Anchorage

nchorage, Alaska is the largest city in the state, home to just under 270,000 people (almost half the state's population). At a glance, it looks like any other small city in the United States, a bustling little metropolis that serves as a huge tourist hub. Located in the heart of Southcentral Alaska, it's surrounded by a beautiful backdrop of ocean and mountains, mild weather, and a surprisingly urban vibe.

Anchorage was settled by the Athabascan Dena'ina natives possibly as early as 500 AD, and they were the first point of contact for later explorers. By the late 1800s, the area had been settled by Russians, however it is English explorer Captain James Cook who is given credit for Alaska's discovery. Over the next hundred years, the area continued to grow with Russian trading, gold mining along Turnagain Arm, and the eventual startup of the Alaska Railroad.

But there is more to the city of Anchorage than meets the eye. Underneath the surface of this urban setting, the stories that go along with the history are often unsettling. Anchorage itself started as a tent city created to support the railroad back in 1913. Laws were often made up as one went along and people did what they wanted. Even today, Alaska is considered a place where a person can go to "disappear," an idea that has brought in a wealth of shady characters over the years. Red light districts, bootlegging, mob activity, drug running, and violence were all part of Anchorage's history.

People come to Alaska to explore their wild side, to get away from polite society, and immerse themselves in a place that has never fully succumbed to convention. Anchorage is no different. It might look like a mini-Seattle with a coffee house on every corner, have plenty of shopping and an active nightlife, but it's that frontier history and violent past that makes it unique.

There are several places within the municipality of Anchorage that have ghost stories attached. I chose some of the oldest buildings in the area, as well as those with the most colorful histories and that are known for ghost sightings. I was also lucky enough to meet up with a local paranormal investigation group, who helped me immensely in my research.

††††††††††††

Historic Anchorage Hotel

The Historic Anchorage Hotel is one of the oldest standing buildings in Anchorage. Originally built in 1916, it's the only historic hotel among Anchorage's hotel choices. In 1936, an addition to the hotel was built, with a walkway between the two. The 1964 earthquake effectively destroyed the original building, leaving just the 1936 addition standing on its own.

The lobby of the Historic Anchorage Hotel, where many paranormal incidents have occurred. *Photo by Jody Ellis-Knapp.*

Historic Anchorage Hotel, room 205, one of the more active rooms.
Photo by Jody Ellis-Knapp.

The occurrences at the Historic Anchorage Hotel are enough to make even the most adamant non-believer re-think their views on the paranormal. Terri Russi has been the General Manager of the hotel since 2004 and says that she always had what she calls a "general belief" in ghosts, but since starting her job at the hotel, that belief has solidified into certainty.

"I am a visual person," she says, "and the things I've seen just cannot be denied."

She has witnessed several incidents while working, as well as heard many stories from guests. Her own experiences include looking in a mirror that hung in the lobby...only to see a black smoky reflection like the train of a dress lingering behind her.

"I thought there was a fire," she says, "but when I turned around, there was nothing there. That same day, I saw a lamp in the lobby encircled by the same black smoke. Again, I thought the lamp was on fire, but it wasn't and the smoke soon disappeared."

Russi says that there is a picture of the famed Alaskan artist Sydney Lawrence, who often stayed at the hotel, on the mantle of the lobby's fireplace. One quiet afternoon, the picture flew off the mantel of its own accord and fell to the ground, breaking the frame. There are also stories of a bottle of scotch regularly flying off the shelf when they had an attached bar in the hotel.

The scotch, says Russi, is probably coming from the ghost of John Sturgis, who was the first police chief of Anchorage. He was shot in a back alley behind the hotel, supposedly with his own handgun, and died at the local hospital before he could name his killer. The killer was never captured and Sturgis' ghost has never found peace. Since that time, events at the hotel have led people to believe that Sturgis has made the hotel his personal haunting grounds. There are often sightings and incidents on the anniversary of his death, such as one employee who said they were in the basement during the wee hours of the morning. As they came up the stairs to the front desk, there was an apparition right in front of the elevator. It was gone very quickly and they could not determine any features, but it made that admittedly skeptical employee a believer!

Other supposed ghosts at the hotel include a jilted bride who checked into the hotel on her wedding night and committed suicide, and the ghost of a little boy who drowned in a hotel bathtub. Guests have often called down to the front desk, complaining of children running and yelling in the hallway, when there were no children staying at the hotel. In 2006, a guest staying in room 215 reported that they saw a small boy sitting in front of the door, blocking the entry. Again, there were no children staying in the hotel at that time.

The most active rooms are 205 and 215, as well as the lobby. Russi states that she knows guests have experienced something when they approach the front desk asking, "Are you guys haunted?" One guest was standing in the lobby and suddenly started laughing, and then asked that much-repeated question. "She said she was standing there and could feel someone pushing against her, but there was no one behind her," says Russi.

Over the years, hotel employees have started tracking all of the strange incidents at the hotel and have compiled a 'Ghostly Encounters Journal' in which guests can record things they've experienced. In addition to the occurrences mentioned above, guests have reported voices, lights turning on and off of their own accord, and one guest said she went out for awhile and when she came back, someone had used a water glass in her room and the soap had been opened but not used. Guests have also reported seeing figures in "old fashioned clothing" in their rooms and one man said that while he was sleeping, he woke to the feeling of someone sitting on top of him.

Other incidents include doors opening at random, items flying off counters, and the smell of something burning. A guest staying in room 304 said her television came on by itself one night, and the occupants of room 207 kept hearing someone knock on the door but when they would open the door, no one was there.

Some guests have set up timed tape recorders in the interest of charting the activity at the hotel. One year at Halloween, two women tape-recorded the activity in room 205. On the tape, you can hear the ladies talking to each other in the background, but then you hear very loud breathing. Then a voice says, "Don't move that." The voice then said "Chocolate" and you could hear a wrapper being opened.

The Historic Anchorage Hotel seems to be a popular guesthouse for the living and a gateway to the spirit world. While the hauntings here all seem to be mild and the ghosts do not appear to mean any harm, there are certainly a large number of ghostly guests who don't seem interested in "checking out."

~~~~~

Club Paris

It makes sense that a building that once housed a funeral home would have some spiritual activity lurking about. This is the case with Club Paris, one of Anchorage's premier restaurants and also one of the oldest establishments in the city.

Club Paris opened in the late 1950s in downtown Anchorage. It was built in 1936 as the Carlquist-Menzel Funeral Parlor back when the streets were still dirt roads and Anchorage was more of a frontier town than a city. When the restaurant opened, it quickly became a popular place and is still known to have the best steaks in town today. It's considered an upscale restaurant and is frequented by many of Anchorage's elite.

Club Paris bar area, where things regularly seem to fly off the bar and onto the floor. *Photo by Jody Ellis-Knapp.*

Other than a few moderate upgrades and enhancements, not much has changed inside the restaurant and it still gives one the feeling of old time Alaska. With low lights and dark wood, the only thing missing is a haze of cigar smoke, which is no longer part of the ambience since the city's restaurants became smoke free.

Stan Selman owns Club Paris with his brother Scott. They, along with their sister Sheila, inherited the place from their father Charlie

Club Paris hallway to the ladies restroom, where the ghost "Emily" has been seen lurking. *Photo by Jody Ellis-Knapp.*

when he passed away. Charlie Selman purchased the restaurant from Frank Taylor and Jack Higgins, who were actually the second owners. Tommy Strachan originally started Club Paris, along with a partner named Mary Powell. According to Selman, Strachan had a drinking and gambling problem and it was up to Mary to keep him from emptying the till—a job she apparently took very seriously.

Club Paris restaurant booth, where you may have an unlikely guest join you for dinner!
Photo by Jody Ellis-Knapp.

"One day I was standing at the bar, and from the corner of my eye, I saw a woman standing at the till. She had long hair, a blouse and a long skirt on," he says. "When I turned around to look more fully, no one was there."

Selman supposes it's Mary, still checking the till.

The bar seems to be the hub of paranormal activity.

"I work nights most of the time and I'm here by myself a lot," says Stan. "Plenty of times, I've walked by the bar and things just fly off it onto the floor. I finally brought a level in to see if the bar was crooked! But it's perfectly level. I don't know how to explain it."

Club Paris employees said that they were all recently standing around chatting before opening one day, when a bottle of Worcestershire sauce suddenly flew off the counter behind the bar and shattered on the floor. No one was near it and all the employees saw it happen.

"It was really weird!" says Selman. "There is definitely *something* going on."

When asked if he believes in ghosts, Selman is diplomatic. "Well," he says, "I figure our bodies are composed of energy. Everything really, is energy. When we die, I just can't believe that energy dies too. Some has to be left over and it makes sense that it would somehow congregate in certain areas."

Another female ghost, dubbed "Emily" by the employees, has been seen lurking around the hallway that leads to the restrooms. Long time employee Julie Dale says she often sees "Emily" peripherally, standing near the hostess station. When asked if she was frightened by such a presence, Dale smiles and says, "I think she just likes to watch and see what's going on."

~~~~~

4th Avenue Theatre

Anchorage's 4th Avenue Theatre was built in 1947, in the heart of the downtown district. It was originally constructed and owned by Austin Eugene Lathrop, an entrepreneur who came to Alaska in 1896 as part owner and pilot of a steam schooner. He was one of the first oil prospectors in the state, drilling for oil in Cold Bay, Alaska.

Lathrop was heavily involved in the arts scene in Alaska. He built movie theaters in Cordova, Fairbanks, and Anchorage in the early 1900s, purchased the *Fairbanks Daily News-Miner* newspaper, and started the first radio station, KFAR, in Alaska's interior. He actually broke ground for the 4th Avenue Theatre in 1941, but World War II put a halt to construction and the theatre was not completed until the war ended.

The theatre used to be one of the hotspots of Anchorage, with feature films shown regularly to sold-out crowds. It managed to survive Alaska's 1964 earthquake, emerging relatively unscathed from the disaster. It was placed on the National Registry of Historic Places in 1981, and continued to show first run movies until 1985, when the movie "The Goonies" finished its run there. The theatre closed down soon after. It enjoyed a brief revival as a gift shop in the early 1990s when real estate investor Robert Gottstein purchased it, but it was put back on the market in 2005.

The ghosts that haunt the theatre are reported to be benign presences that only appear periodically. The main ghost story circles around a little girl who fell from the balcony of the theatre to her death. Guests of the theatre have reported seeing her sitting in the balcony. There are also rumors of a "womanly presence" seen drifting in various parts of the theatre, but no one has determined who this woman might be.

The theatre sits empty today, a legacy of faded grandeur, in disrepair, and facing an uncertain future. It seems destined to become a ghost itself, as it sits vacant year after year ... a sad ending, perhaps, for a theatre that managed to survive a major earthquake, wars, and several owners.

~~~~~

4th Avenue Theater... A classic piece of Anchorage's history. *Photo by Jody Ellis-Knapp.*

Clark Middle School

Originally built in 1959, Clark Middle School, located in east Anchorage off Bragaw Street, was constructed out of concrete block and steel, and was intended for use as a fallout shelter as well as a school. This was in the midst of the Cold War, with many U.S. citizens concerned that Russia would attack any day.

The school was named after Orah Dee Clark, the first principal and superintendent of Anchorage schools. Clark was a teacher and principal back in 1915, when teachers could not marry and either had to quit when they did marry, or commit to staying single as a career teacher. Clark often visited her namesake school during its early years, chatting with students and teachers and making her presence known.

Miss Clark may have continued to make her presence known after her death, and her commitment to education seems to have transcended the grave, for the old school is long thought to be haunted. Both students and teachers alike have told stories of a woman in a white dress wandering the halls. Strange occurrences – such as musical instruments making noise with no one in the room and lights turning on and off – add to the mystery of the school. Some teachers at the school have been known to tell students there is a female ghost who comes up through the floor from the basement while other teachers and students say its nothing more than a story.

Today, Clark Middle School is under construction; its original plumbing and electrical wiring is worn out, and the school itself is too small to accommodate a growing student population. It will be interesting to see if the ghostly "lady in white" will re-enter the new school, making her benign presence known, or if she will find another residence to haunt.

~~~~~

Courtyard by Marriott

By any standards, the Courtyard by Marriott, located in Spenard, near the Anchorage Airport, is a fairly young hotel to have a ghost. Built in 1997, the hotel boasts 154 rooms and appears to be a standard, non-descript hotel, perfect for business travelers, modern, and in a convenient location.

Yet guests of room 201 have reported unusual activity there. From feeling a presence in the room, to lights going on and off, and things being moved around, the ghost of a man who died there — and whose body was not found for several days — is believed to be haunting it. Research of newspaper archives yield nothing in regards to this story, yet all the same, something in the room leaves guests unsettled and employees shaken.

Stories and rumors also circulate about a mysterious ghost that wanders the parking lot of the hotel, and, of all things, a cat ghost that likes to visit rooms 103 and 107. Why the spirit of a cat would remain in a hotel, a place where cats are most likely not even allowed, is unknown. Perhaps it gives constant chase to a ghostly mouse?

~~~~~

Courtyard by Marriott... This Anchorage hotel is located in Spenard and supposedly has a resident ghost and even a ghost-cat!
Photo by Jody Ellis-Knapp.

Ship Creek

Located in downtown Anchorage, with the main artery running through the shipyards and railroad areas, Ship Creek is a popular tourist destination in the summer, as well as a fun and easy place to do some salmon fishing. Creating a picturesque backdrop amidst Anchorage's industrial district, it's a seemingly innocuous area. Many of Anchorage's homeless tend to congregate along the creek, perhaps because it's a small touch of nature in an urban environment, a peaceful respite from an otherwise unsettling daily life. Unfortunately, this tiny corner of natural Alaska beauty has also been a part of the darker side of Anchorage, with violent acts such as rape, fighting, drinking and drug use, and even murder taking place on these outwardly placid shores.

Ship Creek in Anchorage...where a sense of mystery and foreboding permeates the air.
Photo by Jody Ellis-Knapp.

While those who hang out around Ship Creek refuse to speak of it or even acknowledge it, there is a story of a woman who was murdered there over twenty years ago—and whose spirit remains behind and warns other homeless women away from the area. Unfortunately, she has not always been able to caution women as much as she might hope to, for other murders have taken place near and around Ship Creek, including one in 2002. Raped and then stabbed to death, the body of Cynthia Henry was found under Anchorage's A Street Bridge, near the creek. That murder was eventually solved, but others, such as the case of a woman named Vera Hapoff who was found dead in Ship Creek in 1999 under suspicious circumstances, were never resolved.

There have also been numerous deaths in or near the creek that have been deemed accidental. In 1997, a man, who had been drinking heavily, waded into the creek, fell, and drowned. There have been overdoses, hypothermia, and near misses with people coming very close to meeting their demise at the creek.

The question comes to mind; is there some kind of evil entity that lurks around the creek itself, driving people to commit unspeakable acts? Or is it just the combination of many homeless camps and alcohol-infused, random happenings near what can be a dangerous waterway? Looking closer at the rushing waters of the creek, one might see shadows lying under the surface, hear whispers under the serene sounds of a burbling creek, or feel a sense of foreboding surrounding the vicinity.

While tourists fish and salmon spawn, what else might be spawning beneath the murky surface of Anchorage's Ship Creek?

~~~~~

Northern Lights Hotel

The now-defunct Northern Lights Hotel got it start in 1965 under the name Gold Rush Motor Lodge. This was a seventy-four-room, wood frame motel—nothing fancy even by Alaska standards. In January 1970, there was a fire, thought to be arson, which left five guests dead. That was only the beginning of what turned into an incredibly long run of bad luck.

The hotel was rebuilt after the fire, and was purported to be the first hotel in Alaska with a color television in every room. Shortly after its re-opening, it was shut down by the Internal Revenue Service.

Open again, new owners tried to make it a more upscale hotel, but a string of fires that caused hundreds of thousands of dollars in damage eventually pushed them into bankruptcy in 1979. The hotel was re-branded as a Ramada, functioning as such until Cusack Development Inc. purchased it in 1994. They renamed it the Northern Lights Hotel and opened Cusack's Brew Pub on the ground floor. The pub was very popular with the hockey crowd, filled to capacity on a regular basis. This upswing of success was short-lived however; in 2000, the pub briefly lost its liquor license due to unpaid taxes and Cusack filed for bankruptcy protection just two years later.

Since then, the hotel has been used as a training ground by the Anchorage Police Department, unable to operate as a hotel again until all legal issues have been resolved.

With such bad luck, some say the hotel itself is cursed, and those who worked at the hotel when it was open have had many run-ins with decidedly unfriendly spirits. Hotel guests also often complained about noises in empty rooms and have reported seeing apparitions wandering the hallways. One person tells of attempting to walk into an empty room one evening, late at night. He started to open the door and found it blocked—it would only open a few inches. He pushed on it, thinking that something must be wedged in front of it. As he pushed on it, it opened up about a foot and then slammed shut, as if pushed by a large gust of wind. He later attempted to open the same door...and it opened fine, the room was empty, there was nothing blocking the door, and no windows were open to cause a gust of wind.

Rick Thayer, chief investigator for Mystery Alaska Research Society, used to work security at the hotel. He says, "Things would get moved around. Once a phone flew across the room, out of nowhere. Doors would slam shut and lights would turn on and off when there was no one in the hotel besides us." Thayer says that his experiences at the hotel were some of the first ghost encounters he ever had, which helped lead him towards his pursuit of paranormal investigations.

Northern Lights Hotel...Once a premiere Anchorage Hotel, this haunted hotspot now sits empty. *Photo by Jody Ellis-Knapp.*

Northern Lights Hotel...an eerie window into a supposedly haunted room.
Photo by Jody Ellis-Knapp.

Chapter Two
Eagle River / Chugiak

The Eagle River/Chugiak area is located just outside Anchorage and is part of the Anchorage municipality. With roughly 30,000 people, this is a larger suburb of the city. It's country living at its finest, yet is close enough to the city to make it appealing to commuters. It includes the outlying areas of Birchwood, Peter's Creek, Thunderbird Falls, and Eklutna.

The land was originally occupied by Tanaina Athabascan Indians, in the area that eventually became the village of Eklutna, but homesteaders eventually settled it as an agricultural community. In 1975, it became part of the Anchorage municipality, despite strong opposition from many local residents.

Today, this is one of the fastest growing places in the Southcentral community. It's a place where those who are tired of the busy city life of Anchorage can escape, while still having a reasonable drive to work each day. It's a tight-knit community with a defined small town feel, a hallmark of that strong independent spirit that makes Alaska so special.

There are many old stories about ghosts around here; some more realistic than others, and some that have even supposedly been proven true! But whether fact or legend, the stories embody the history of Alaska and the people who call it home.

†††††††††††

Birchwood Saloon

Birchwood Saloon is located approximately twenty miles north of Anchorage, just off Glenn Highway at the North Birchwood exit. A nondescript building, it houses a small bar and liquor store. Locals gather every weekend to have a few drinks and relax, but there are also a host of permanent residents who don't imbibe in liquor or conversation—at least not from our world.

The bar at the Birchwood Saloon, a hotbed of paranormal activity.
Photo by Jody Ellis-Knapp.

The pool tables at the Birchwood Saloon. Investigators heard the sound of pool balls being hit when they played back recordings they had made. *Photo by Jody Ellis-Knapp.*

Wanda Gates has owned the saloon for fifteen years. She started there as the bookkeeper for the previous owner and, when the original owner's health left her unable to keep the place, Wanda bought it.

"I never believed any of the stories when I first bought the place," she says, "but as time went on and I kept seeing things and different things were happening, I started to realize there was something to it."

A man died under what were deemed suspicious circumstances back in 1980. His name was Jack Atwater and he was working on the roof of the building, then known as the Pilot's Grille restaurant and Mt. McKinley View Lounge. His father Galen was the owner of the business at that time. The story isn't totally clear as to why Jack was on the roof. Early newspaper reports say he was shoveling snow. Other reports say he was installing an antenna. Regardless, he somehow got tangled in some low hanging wires and was electrocuted, subsequently catching on fire. He suffered third degree burns over forty percent of his body and later died at Providence Hospital.

"I'm sure the ghost I see is Jack," says Gates. "I knew him before he died and I know it's him."

Since then, the building has had a series of ongoing paranormal occurrences:

† patrons report seeing a person out of the corner of their eye ... yet *no one* is there when they turn around;

† pool balls clack across the table with *no one* touching them;

† and footsteps are heard on the roof, yet the roof is clear when people run out to look

†††††

"I usually see something about once a week," says Wanda. "Sometimes it's a shadow out of the corner of my eye; sometimes it's a man walking around in a blue flannel shirt and jeans. Once in awhile it still startles me, but the ghost here is more of a jokester. I've never felt any kind of threat."

Not all of the people working there have felt the same, however. Gates has had one bartender quit because she couldn't handle it. "But all my other employees have gotten used to it," she says. "I don't really tell people about it when I first hire them, because it can scare them off. My newest bartender had never heard anything about the place when she started. She came to me and said she'd been seeing things...had some incidents where she shut off the lights and then they came back on, and she wondered what was going on!"

When asked if she has ever had any bad experiences with her poltergeist, Gates says, "There was one time, I was in the back room and it suddenly filled with this metallic smell and it got very cold. I got a bad feeling and immediately walked into the other room. That's the only time though."

Gates has gotten so used to the ghosts of the saloon that she sees "Jack" as more of a companion and friend. "I tell him good morning when I come in every day," she laughs.

~~~~~

Eklutna Village National Park

Russian settlers and missionaries brought the Russian Orthodox religion to Alaska. One of the remnants of this history is Eklutna Village National Park. Located twenty-four miles north of Anchorage, en route to the Matanuska-Susitna Valley, this is one of the last villages that existed prior to the influx of American settlers. Today the Eklutna area is still inhabited by some of the original tribal descendents and has a population of about seventy people.

Eklutna...Spirit House at the Eklutna Cemetery, intended to house the belongings and spirit of those who have passed. *Photo by Jody Ellis-Knapp*.

Eklutna Spirit houses..wandering ghosts have been seen here, those not satisfied with the spirit houses built for them. *Photo by Jody Ellis-Knapp.*

The Eklutna Cemetery shows the blending of the Russian Orthodox roots and native history, with brightly colored spirit houses. These houses were constructed to keep wandering spirits confined and are erected on top of the gravesites. They also contain personal items that belonged to the deceased.

The cemetery brings in many tourists who want to see the unique and beautifully colored spirit houses. The village also has a museum, gift shop, and is the site of the St. Nicholas Russian Orthodox Church. The church was built in the 1830s and, while no longer used for services, still contains many of the original icons and historic pieces.

Eklutna..The welcome sign in front of the church at Eklutna cemetery.
Photo by Jody Ellis-Knapp.

Apparently, the Spirit Houses *haven't* kept those wandering ghosts confined as much as was hoped. People believe the spirits of native ancestors still wander the cemetery; those not pleased with their houses and who are searching for the belongings they left behind. Some residents claim that screams and voices can be heard in the cemetery late at night, as well as a ghostly figure that seems to be looking for its own spirit house.

~~~~~

Chugiak's Badarka Road

Chugiak, Alaska is located outside the city of Anchorage. An off-shoot of Eagle River, it's a part of the Anchorage municipality. Badarka Road, located off Birchwood Loop Road, is the site of a haunting that is chilling, yet also heartbreaking.

As the story goes, a small girl and her father were in the woods near the road, chopping wood for their cabin. The father had lodged an ax in a nearby tree, up high where he thought the child would not be able to reach it. While her father was resting for a moment, the girl decided to pull the ax out and chop some wood too. As the ax came out of the tree, it hit her in the head, killing her instantly. The father apparently stayed with her, dying himself of hypothermia.

If one drives out about halfway down the road at precisely 3:30 a.m., there is supposedly an apparition of the father holding his dead child that can be seen, sitting in the middle of the road. Yet many people have tried driving out to Bardarka Road to investigate, but the road is incredibly difficult to find.

A local man said it's right off Birchwood Loop Road in the Chugiak area, and is easy to find during the day. But those who try driving out there at night can't seem to find the road and end up lost. Another person said that a group of them drove out that way late one night in order to try to catch a glimpse of the apparition. Familiar with the area, it should have been an easy and quick drive. But they ended up getting turned around, again and again. Every time they turned down what they thought was the correct road, they would end up at a dead end, or end up in a different neighborhood. After two hours of seeking the elusive road, they gave up.

Chapter Three

MatanuskaSusitna Valley

The Matanuska-Susitna Valley sits north of Anchorage, roughly fifty miles up the highway. Originally inhabited by the Dena'ina tribe, it became a settlement with the arrival of the railroad in 1916, serving early miners and trappers who sought out gold.

During the 1930s, it was named part of Roosevelt's "New Deal," in which 203 families were offered a chance at a new life as farmers in Alaska, an escape from the Great Depression. Homesteaders made their way to the valley, quickly establishing themselves and creating a functional colony and farming co-op.

Today "The Valley," as it's locally known, consists of the towns Wasilla and Palmer and the outlying areas of Willow, Talkeetna, and the Butte. Now holding a population of over 80,000 people, it has grown a lot from those colony days of the 1930s. There are still many active farms, and the lifestyle here is rural Alaska at its best. Tourists engulf the area during the summer months, enjoying fishing, camping, and hiking, as well as exploring the history that abounds here. Winter activities include snow machining and winter camping, as well as being the starting point for the last great race, the Iditarod.

Of course, a history such as this is bound to generate a few ghost stories. With gold mining and the railroad bringing in all kinds of somewhat unsavory characters, the Matanuska-Susitna Valley certainly had its fair share of crime and violence. A violent death always seems to leave a spirit unhappy, making it want to remain behind once life has left the human body. Or if someone dies under unusual circumstances, perhaps not murder but just a strange accident…that's when stories seem to surface about spirits not at rest. There is always the possibility that a person didn't die under shadowy circumstances, but just had unfinished business in this world. Maybe they are trying to find some closure, so they can move on to the next level.

††††††††††††

KeplerBradley Lakes State Recreation Area

Sitting 3.6 miles from the town of Palmer, this is a popular little fishing hole enjoyed by tourists and locals alike. During the day, it's relaxing and offers some of the best trails, trout fishing, and camping in the area.

But late at night, especially during the off-season, something (or someone) else has decided to "camp" here. There are those who claim that the ghost of a man who was shot here many years ago occasionally makes his presence known, with some campers claiming to have seen him, dragging someone through the bushes. No one knows for sure what kind of violence may have occurred here, but the man looks to have been shot and is wild eyed and angry.

He is best *seen* during the hours of midnight and 3 a.m. — yet makes *no* noise or disturbance. Those who have seen him say that while the apparition is unnerving, they never get a sense of fear or danger from him. If anything, it's a huge feeling of sorrow and loss.

~~~~~

Motherlode Lodge

Located north of Palmer, the Motherlode Lodge sits in the heart of Hatcher's Pass, a natural resort area that is heavily populated by tourists in the summer and skiers and snowmachiners in the winter.

Reproductive drawing of Motherlode Lodge by Benjamin A. Ellis.

The lodge was originally built in 1942 by Victor Cotinni, and with the addition of a ski tow, became a stopping point for workers of the nearby Independence Mine. Cotinni named it the Little Susitna Lodge as it sat next to the river. After the mine shut down in the 1950s, the property was purchased by Bill Betts, who operated it as a resort lodge with his wife. It later closed completely in 1987, but reopened under new ownership in 1991 and was renamed Motherlode Lodge. Currently managed by Carol Hart and her family, it remains a popular resort and vacation area for tourists and locals alike.

According to local stories, Motherlode Lodge not only hosts tourists, but also a rather active assortment of entities and spirits. Reports by both patrons and staff include various kinds of paranormal activity. They include:

† guests seeing a man standing behind them when they look in the front hallway mirror, but when they turn around, no one is there;

† cabinets opening and closing on their own in the bar area and footsteps running overhead;

† a red floating gown drifting along an upper landing;

† housekeepers making up the bed in Room 12...only to come back later and find it disheveled

†††††

Manager Carol Hart has been running the lodge since April 2007, and says she's not a firm believer in the paranormal. "I have all of my doubts and questions in regards to that," she says. "However there have been a couple of experiences that I have considered inexplicable."

Hart says that while there have been many tales over the years as far as ghost sightings, she sees it more as an aura or presence that occupies the place. "If you will, there is some type of presence in the lodge that is warm, inviting, and friendly. It is very hard work at this lodge, and there have been times I felt so tired and so run down, and somehow I get a feeling of something embracing me and telling me to go on."

Hart tells a story of a personal experience she had with this entity:

"We decided to renovate the kitchen, with plans to tear out all the electrical that was faulty, pull out old equipment, just re-do everything. We were standing in the kitchen discussing the renovation. I had my back to the kitchen door. It was the start of winter season and it was very cold in the lodge, especially it the kitchen where we tend to keep the temperature low anyway. So the kitchen was chilly and I am standing there discussing the designs I want. Suddenly I felt this embrace, all around my back and down by my hip. It was very warm, and I turned around, thinking that a fan was somehow blowing warm air on me or something. There was nothing there. As I stood there, suddenly all these ideas about things that needed to do with the kitchen started flooding my head. All of a sudden I was coming up with ideas about things I normally wouldn't know about— like electrical changes. What was really strange is the electrician actually said they were good ideas!"

Hart says that later on, in the midst of all these renovations, she was standing in the kitchen in the very same spot she had stood before. "I was really frustrated and overwhelmed with all the work we had left to do," she says. "Suddenly, the same embrace I'd felt before came again, out of nowhere. I turned again, and no one was there. I had actually forgotten about the first embrace by then. The next morning I woke up and had all these great design ideas to do candy apple red accents and use apples in the theme, in an early '30s and '40s style. As I was telling the contractors about my ideas, they were very excited and agreed. At the moment I was telling them about the ideas, the embrace came yet again. I tried to attribute it to a hot flash. But it seems unusual that I only got these hot flashes while standing in one specific area of the kitchen."

There have also been several incidents involving a mirror that sits at the end of a hallway. Says Hart, "The mirror has been there since the '80s or so. One day I was walking through there and glanced up into the mirror. I thought I saw a man walking behind me with a cowboy hat on. I turned to greet him and no one was there. I just figured it was a trick of the mirror, as it is curved. Later that day, I was looking out into the window of the parking lot, and saw the reflection of the same man in the cowboy hat. I thought someone was here to check in. I went outside and no one was there. I asked one of the cooks who had just arrived if he had seen anyone, and he said, 'No one.'"

Just a few days later, Hart says a server approached her and asked, "Do you know where that man went?" Hart said she hadn't seen any man. The server said a man in a cowboy hat had followed her towards the dining room, but she couldn't find him when she went to see where he had seated himself. That same day, a woman came in and wanted to go look at the banquet room. When she came downstairs, she told Hart that a man had just followed her into the bar. Hart investigated and found no one there. The woman later said that she had seen the man walking behind her when she had looked in the hall mirror.

Hart says the man in the mirror seems to be the most consistent story...as told by a number of guests. "They always say they saw a man behind them in the mirror, in a cowboy hat. He appears to have dark skin. I don't ever tell people anything about the mirror because I want to hear what they think. But if someone says they saw someone walking behind them, they always say he was in the mirror and it is a man with a cowboy hat."

Reports of footsteps in the rooms upstairs have often been claimed by both guests and employees. "One night I was standing at the bar with two couples. It was near closing, and we suddenly heard footsteps running around upstairs. It sounded like children running. I blamed it on our two cats, which often ran around up there. One of the couples pointed out the cats, sitting on a nearby window ledge. I then tried to blame it on our dog, which was known to run around up there too. They said 'this dog?' and pointed at the dog, who was lying curled up on the floor under a table. I went upstairs and checked all the rooms, but no one was there. That was one thing I never could explain."

When asked what was one of the most disturbing and unusual experiences she'd had, Hart tells the story of the sad bride.

"We had a wedding planned at the lodge one evening. The bride came in, and out of the thirty plus years we've been doing weddings and receptions, I think she was the saddest bride I'd ever met. She didn't get involved in much of the planning; she didn't seem to care. Her family was running the show and she sat on the sidelines. We have a room upstairs that is set up for the bride to get dressed in. She was getting ready up there, and there was just this solemn air about her the whole time—there was no joy. Her cake was delivered downstairs, and she gave me a cake topper with a figurine of a man and woman. I took it downstairs and put it on the cake, walking away to go set up the gift table. As I walked away, I heard something bounce onto the floor, almost like a ball being bounced. I turned, and saw that the cake topper had come off the cake and bounced all the way across the room. There was no damage to the cake, and the topper missed the cake table altogether, shooting right across the floor! I picked it up, washed it off, and put it back on the cake. In the meantime, the wedding guests were arriving and the bride was in the room still getting ready. She was very nervous so I offered her a cup of tea. As I went downstairs to get her tea, one of the groomsmen came up and said that there was a delay because the bride's sister's car had broken down en route to the lodge. Another member of the wedding party was going to stop and pick her up, so it seemed like the problem was solved. Shortly thereafter, he came to me again and said that the person going to pick up the bride's sister had called— her car had broken down in the exact same place! While they were trying to find someone else to drive down and get them, I took the bride her tea. As she went to take a sip of the tea, the cup slipped and the tea went right down the front of her dress."

Hart concedes that the wedding did go on that day, but she thought the events, coupled with the sadness of the bride, made for a very strange story.

Despite all of her experiences with odd occurrences in the lodge over the years, Hart still considers herself a skeptic. "I do think there is some kind of power out there somewhere," she says, "but I don't think there are ghosts. And even if there are, I don't think they are powerful enough to harm a person. I don't know if I believe in ghosts. I stay at the lodge alone quite often; it doesn't scare me at all. But I do get a sense of such warmth there; I do have to wonder sometimes just what that might be."

~~~~~

Knik Road

Knik Road, which used to be not much more than a trail, is a major modern thoroughfare in Wasilla these days. New homes have turned a quiet country road into a busy highway, with those who want to escape the hectic pace of Anchorage creating another level of havoc in a different way. Unfortunately, it seems that the construction of these new residences has left some other residents very disgruntled.

Apparently, the whole area was once an Athabascan graveyard. In 2006, ancient bones were discovered, eroded out of the bank along Cook Inlet. There are ancient graves scattered all over the Knik area, most of them unmarked and unknown. Gravesites have been discovered over the years, with long time residents fighting hard to keep the areas around the graves undisturbed. This has proven to be a daunting task, as the wheels of progress seem to want to keep on building rather than preserve these ancient resting places.

The paranormal investigators of the group IOPIA say they have received calls from people living in the new houses along Knik Road—houses never occupied by anyone else—and they are *seeing* apparitions in the houses. Some people believe that there are old gravesites that have been disturbed, creating unrest in the spirit world and an influx of hauntings. Traditional Athabascan beliefs say that if a grave is disturbed, that person's spirit will wander the earth until they are re-buried and ceremonially put to rest. Some think that respecting this tradition and maintaining protection of the ancient burial grounds will help keep the ancestors spirits happy and at peace.

Chapter Four

Talkeetna

Long before the city of Anchorage came into existence, Talkeetna was an established mining town. Like many of Alaska's small towns, Talkeetna's roots originally come from the Alaskan natives who settled there. Talkeetna, meaning "river of plenty," was named thus by the Dena'ina Indians as the town has three rivers that meet in it—the Susitna, the Chulitna, and the Talkeetna. In the 1890s, it was set up as a trading station and the discovery of gold in 1892 brought in the miners and money-seekers, turning this tiny village into a lively little town. The official town site was established in 1919.

Located 120 miles from Anchorage, Talkeetna today is a busy tourist destination in the summer, with fishing, hunting, and flight-seeing operations on nearly every corner. It's also known around the world as a base camp for climbers attempting to conquer nearby Denali (officially known as Mt. McKinley). Much quieter in winter, it's home mostly to locals who spend the colder months telling tales and having a beer or two, while their dogs roam free both inside the various watering holes and out. With a population of seven hundred plus people, this is a friendly place where a frontier lifestyle still exists.

A huge portion of Talkeetna's downtown area was added to the National Registry of Historic Places in 1993. With so many old buildings and such a wealth of history, it makes sense that Talkeetna is thought to be haunted. There are plenty of ghost stories told around the fire in the dead of winter. A few in particular seem to come up again and again, leaving one wondering if there just might be some real spirits hanging around long past tourist season.

††††††††††††

Talkeetna Landings Bed and Breakfast

Located between 2nd and 3rd Streets in downtown Talkeetna, this bed and breakfast is owned by Gale, John, and Genna Moses and has been in operation since the year 2000. Previous owners have reported strange noises coming from the basement, as well as footsteps echoing through the house. Doors opening and closing — one former resident says she actually *saw* the doorknob to the basement door turn and the door open, as well as items being found moved from one place to another.

Apparently the original cabin of the house was built by a gold miner who fell in love with a showgirl who subsequently left him. He died penniless and alone in the cabin. When they brought his body in to be buried, they dug the grave and then tried holding the burial the following day. Because Talkeetna gets a lot of rain, there was about two feet of water in the open grave. Supposedly the residents had to throw rocks on the casket to hold it down during the service, as it kept trying to rise up with the water. The miner had a daughter, and he had asked his daughter to bury him with his late wife in another state. The daughter, eager and greedy to take over his land, did not honor his request. The miner has apparently stayed around, angry at the lack of dignity in his burial and his daughter's treachery.

There is another story of a pilot who owned the property at one time. He had to retrieve the bodies of some climbers that had perished on Denali. As it was the middle of winter and the ground was frozen, the bodies were stored in the basement of the cabin until they could be properly buried. Many of the ghost stories associated with the cabin seem to originate with the basement—perhaps the men who died on that mountain are still there.

Owner John Moses says nothing has ever happened to him personally and he has never had guests say anything to him about it either.

"We do have a creepy basement," he says, "but it's just a basement. The scariest thing that has happened to me in regards to the basement is it flooding awhile back!"

Moses states that the stories of bodies in the basement are just that—stories. "The basement wasn't even built until the late '60s to early '70s, so I doubt that there were ever any bodies stowed there."

While he considers himself a skeptic, he does accept the possibility of the paranormal.

"I used to work for a newspaper in San Francisco," Moses says. "The building it was housed in was supposed to be haunted and we had weird stuff happen all the time. One night I was working late and a mirror in the bathroom came flying off the wall and shattered. I left right away!"

Moses says they did have a dresser in the Bed and Breakfast that used to tip over all the time, but once he moved it to a different location that stopped, so he chalks it up to an uneven floor in an old building.

"The only kind of strange thing that ever happened to me was one time I was talking to my sister about how the place is supposed to be haunted. The clock that was hanging on the wall happened to fall on the floor just at that moment. Of course, I had just hung the clock the day before, so it may have just been me not hanging it properly."

The stories do not seem likely to die, but Moses laughs them off, saying, "I see this as a warm and happy place, so if we do have any ghosts around, *they* are friendly and happy ones."

~~~~~

Talkeetna Roadhouse

Talkeetna Roadhouse was originally built between 1914 and 1917. One of downtown Talkeetna's oldest establishments, it's famous for its bakery and hospitable atmosphere.

Stories have surfaced of some unusual happenings in the Roadhouse, such as *drifting whispers* heard in a hallway, *creaking footsteps* in rooms that are not occupied, and *feelings* of a presence when no one else is in the room.

Owner Trisha Costello has had the place since 1996 and is the seventh owner since its inception. She says that she has never seen or heard anything that she deems unexplainable. As far as she knows, no one has died in the Roadhouse nor has anything violent happened there that might leave behind spiritual unrest.

"When people ask if the place is haunted, I have to be honest and say, 'I don't think so,'" says Costello.

However, Costello also adds, "When I first got the place, I sometimes felt like someone was standing behind me or watching me when no one was there. I do think this was more of a personal thing as my grandfather had recently died and I was still dealing with that. I also spend a lot of time in the bakery in the very early mornings. At 2 a.m. I am often the only one here, which makes it easy to freak yourself out. As a Roadhouse, we never really close, which means that we can have guests coming in at all hours, causing the occasional weird thing to happen, but nothing that cannot be explained."

Costello says that she has never had a guest approach her about any specific ghost sightings, but the mere age of the place may be partially to blame for the rumors and stories. "The place creaks," she says. "You walk in one section and it creaks in another section. It is such an old building and has so many add-ons to it that it isn't surprising that there are odd noises and weird sounds."

It's possible that the rumors about Talkeetna Roadhouse are nothing but tall tales ... the product of an overactive imagination. Costello says she remains open to the idea of spirits, even if there aren't any in her lodge.

"If there happens to be a homeless ghost out there that might want to stay, as long as they are kind and gentle and like kids, I welcome them! I could always use the extra help in the bakery!" she laughs.

~~~~~

Fairview Inn

Built in 1923, Fairview Inn is another building in Talkeetna that is on the National Register of Historic Places. It was originally built by Ben Neuman, who hoped to entice travelers needing accommodations as they traveled along the Alaska Railroad. As the town grew, it became a year-round operation and a popular watering hole.

The Inn's history includes colorful characters and equally colorful owners. A place where locals collaborated and visitors soaked up the atmosphere, its claims to fame include a visit by the twenty-ninth President, Warren Harding, who stopped for a drink at the Fairview Inn while passing through Talkeetna on a visit to Alaska. He died in San Francisco shortly thereafter, and rumors still remain about him being poisoned at the Fairview Inn.

One wall of the Inn is called "Dead Man's Wall" and is a collection of photos of all the climbers that came through and did not survive their ascent of Denali...a rather melancholy assemblage that only adds to the stories of ghosts and poltergeists.

Reports of paranormal activity include footsteps and noises in the upstairs areas, with room 1 being the most active. Locals claim there is a ghost that lives at the Inn, dubbed "Eight Ball," who is the source of most of the strange happenings. While no one could confirm any actual sightings of the ghosts, many say that they do feel a presence there and are sure there is some kind of entity occupying the place.

~~~~~

Talkeetna Cemetery

There is no better place for turbulent spirits than a cemetery—and Talkeetna Cemetery is no exception. With markers dating back to the 1800s, as well as a Climbers museum with a listing of all the mountaineers who perished on Denali, there is a wealth of history here—history and maybe *something* more.

Supposedly, if you go into the cemetery late at night, you can hear a child jumping rope and singing. There have also been incidents of cold blasts of air seemingly coming from nowhere, and a man in a uniform wandering amongst the gravestones, stopping periodically to read them, as if he is looking for something.

While these tales are an interesting part of the folklore surrounding the cemetery, the old gravestones and Climbers museum probably hold more interest to the general public. Locals shrug off the rumors of a haunted cemetery, yet no one wants to hang out there late at night either.

Chapter Five
Kenai Peninsula

The Kenai Peninsula is one of the oldest communities in Alaska. Originally inhabited by the Dena'ina Athabaskan tribe, it was later infiltrated by the Russians for trading and the gold seekers of the Gold Rush days.

The Russian traders arrived in 1791, landing near the mouth of the Kenai River and establishing the first white settlement, Fort St. Nicholas. This was not a peaceful settlement and there was much strife between the settlers and the native people. Murder, rape, and torture occurred at the hands of both parties, until such a time as the authorities had to get involved.

In the late 1880s, a miner prospecting along Turnagain Arm discovered gold. Soon the entire area was flooded with those seeking their fortune—the Gold Rush had begun. The Peninsula soon became a populated area with people settling in and homesteading, and towns springing up.

Today the area includes the towns of Hope, Kenai, Soldotna, Seward, and Homer. All are popular tourist locations and are busy spots for fishing, camping, and hiking in the summer, as well as skiing and snow machining in winter. Many of the historic buildings, relics from the Gold Rush years and the early days, of the area have been preserved—and most have a wealth of interesting stories to go with them.

††††††††††††

Seward

Located 125 miles from Anchorage, the quaint little coastal town of Seward is a quiet and sleepy place during the winter and a hot spot for tourists in the summer. The town sits right on Alaska's Resurrection Bay and is banked by mountains, including the majestic 3,022-foot Mt. Marathon, home to the famous 4th of July Mt. Marathon mountain race. A Russian fur trader and explorer named Alexander Baranof named the Bay.

Seward was originally founded as a railroad camp in 1903 and has a year-round population of just under 3,000 people. The town was named for President Lincoln's Secretary of State, William Henry Seward, who engineered the purchase of Alaska from Russia.

As with most places in Alaska, the history here isn't just rich with folk stories, but true accountings of love, lust, and bad blood. When the railroad arrived, it became a bustling frontier town with street names such as "Millionaire's Row" and "Home Brew Alley." The population rose to upwards of 1,500 people, a huge leap from previous years, creating a housing shortage and overcrowding. By 1920, however, the Alaska Railroad had reduced service to Seward to just one train a week, which brought about economic strife and a sharp drop in population.

Such ups and downs in a town's history are bound to have an affect on the moods and attitudes of the people living there. With economic problems come job losses, money problems, and stress... so it isn't surprising that there has been a history here of love lost, things gone wrong, and murder.

Today, Seward is a major cruise ship port with over 300,000 passengers making their way through the town. It's also a big fishing destination for anglers, and tourists enjoy hiking at the nearby Exit Glacier. But the remnants of a wild past remain, hidden in the darker corners of the town, with the most historic landmarks also displaying the most paranormal activity.

†††††††††††

The Van Gilder Hotel

The Van Gilder Hotel is the oldest surviving hotel in Seward and the second oldest hotel in the state of Alaska. It was opened in 1916 by E. L. Van Gilder, who purchased the property with the intent of erecting an office building. As construction was being completed, they decided to add a third floor of rooms for potential boarders. Due to financial constraints, Van Gilder was forced to sell the property to Charles E. Brown of Brown and Hawkins bank and store, leaving Seward shortly thereafter. In 1917, the property changed hands again, purchased by M. A. Arnold, owner of a successful Seattle bank. It remained an office building with some apartments for four more years and then was purchased by Joseph S. Badger, a former restaurant owner and hotel manager. He converted the building into a full-on hotel, one of the finest known in the area.

As time went on, Seward continued to be considered "the Gateway City," as people passed through by ships, rail, and road on their way to Anchorage and Interior Alaska. During World War II, there was a large military population in the area as well. After the war years, the hotel lost much of its style and its former elegance became faded grandeur. It was a popular pinochle gaming spot, and old timers met in the lobby regularly. In the 1950s, the building was purchased by an Emma Renwald and she renamed it the "Hotel Renwald." The building was sold in the 1960s to Alaskans Bill and Frances O'Brien, who changed the name back to its original.

Frank Irick purchased the property in 1972 and refurbished it. It became a hang out for some of the bigwigs in the area, supposedly catering to the underbelly of Alaska politics. According to current owner Jon Faulkner, some thought it operated as an off-the-map brothel. The first floor was converted into a restaurant by Irick, thought to be set up primarily for social functions and to keep the shadier guests self-contained and out of the public eye. The property eventually fell into foreclosure.

Deenie and Don Nelson bought the property out of bankruptcy from First National Bank of Alaska in the early to mid 1990s. They immediately decommissioned the restaurant, running it as solely a hotel operation.

Jon Faulkner acquired the property in 2002. It was fairly neglected and his first order of business was to complete some extensive cosmetic repairs. New custom furniture, paint crown moldings, and light fixtures being just a few of the changes made. Says Faulkner, "I felt there was a strong marketing opportunity with this hotel. When it was originally built, it was one of the best built structures of its time, and remains so today."

Faulkner says that while he personally has never encountered any ghosts or unusual happenings, his staff and many hotel guests have had experiences that are hard to explain.

The ghost stories begin with the tale of a young woman, Fannie Mae Boughm, who was murdered by her estranged husband in the hotel during the 1950s. Due to a fire that destroyed many records, the official police data from that era is sparse. But the hotel does have a circulating ghost story about Fannie that is supposed to be based on the actual events leading to her death.

The Van Gilder, circa 1920
Courtesy of Resurrection Bay Historical Society

The Van Gilder Hotel in Seward, circa 1920 — Seward's oldest and most haunted hotel. *Photo courtesy of Jon Faulkner*.

James Rowell, who worked at the Van Gilder for a couple years starting in 2005, had some unusual things happen while he was there.

- "The housekeepers would make up the room and would go back to inspect it and someone had been sitting on the bed. They'd leave and hear the shower turn on. Or they would go into a room that was clean and the shower was wet."

††††††

- "One time, I was working the night audit shift, which runs from 11 p.m. to 7 a.m. A lady came down to the front desk at about two in the morning. She said she wanted to know what I was going to do about the woman sitting in the hallway in the rocking chair, banging against the wall. When I went back with her to see what was going on, no one was there. The guest dismissed it, saying the woman must have gone back to her room. But what I found weird was that we do not have a rocking chair in the hotel—not in any of the rooms, not in storage in the basement, nowhere."

††††††

- "I was working the 3 p.m. to 11 p.m. shift, and a young couple was staying in room 306, which just happens to be my favorite room as I think it has the nicest layout in the hotel. The couple had been sleeping all day and were going to go out for dinner. They stopped at the front desk and asked if I wouldn't mind bringing some extra towels to their room. So, I went and got some towels and took them up to the room. I had the master key in my pocket, and as I pulled it from my pocket some money came out with it and fell on the floor. I stuck the key in the lock and bent down to retrieve my money. As I stood up, they key suddenly shot out of the keyhole, across the hallway, and bouncing off the wall. I picked up the key, opened the door to the room very gently, threw the towels in without looking, and shut the door and left! That one really got to me!"

But Rowell's most unsettling experience at the hotel happened one year when they were shutting down for the season.

"It was towards fall and during the off season we have a very minimal staff. We had two housekeepers there and they came downstairs after working all day. I asked if everything was done and they said yes. I told them to go ahead and leave and I would do a final walk-through. I checked the first floor, finishing up with room 112 before I went upstairs to check the other rooms. All the upstairs rooms were fine. I came downstairs and as I entered the hallway, I felt a cold breeze. I thought that maybe the fire escape door had blown open, as that's happened before. As I walked passed room 112, I noticed the door was ajar. I stepped into the room—a room I had just inspected. The bedding was all over the floor, the television was on, and the sink was running in the bathroom. It was simply not possible that someone had been in the room. I cleaned it up, clocked out, and went home!"

†††††

Rowell says that while he considers himself a rational man, he absolutely believes in the paranormal. He says, "I was raised in Atlanta, Georgia. I think that is the most haunted city in the world!" He pauses, and then adds, "You know, I took physics and such in college, but there are *no* explanations I can come up with to make sense of some of the things I've seen."

Jon Faulkner, despite not having any encounters of his own, has had incidents relayed to him that sent chills up his spine.

"There is one story in particular," he says, "a friend of mine, who was working in telecommunications, was working with me in regards to purchasing a new phone system. I had bought a phone system from her before in Seward and wanted to do so again. We were sitting down at the Lands End Resort (Faulkner's other business interest) in Homer to finalize the contract. She told me about one of the first times she met me at the Van Gilder. We were carrying on a conversation and she was sitting in a chair by the door. I was sitting on the couch, talking about phone needs and telecommunications. She asked me if I remembered her suddenly stopping mid-stream in the conversation. I did kind of recall this, but still didn't know where she was going with the story. She said she had looked over towards the front desk and saw a figure standing there in a bowler hat, white shirt, and tie, carrying on his business behind the desk. She told me that she couldn't believe what she had seen and didn't want to say anything to me at the time. I had to admit to myself right then and there that there might be something to the stories. I knew there were people who I respected and seemed reasonable who did believe in ghosts."

When asked if he is still a skeptic, Faulkner laughs and says, "In the end, I tell people that if there is a ghost there, it must be Casper because no one has ever really felt haunted or frightened. I would say experiences lean more towards unusual or weird as opposed to scary. I consider myself open to the experience and yet nothing has happened to me. I guess I don't have the right karma!"

Jesse Lee Home

The Jesse Lee Home for Children is one of Seward's most famous landmarks. Originally started by the Women's Home Missionary School of the Methodist Church back in 1890, it was intended to provide educational services. The facility eventually became an orphanage, housing children who had lost parents or were from broken homes. The school was moved to the outskirts of Seward in 1925, with upwards of seventy children plus employees calling it home.

The Jesse Lee Home was also the residence of one of Alaska's own historical celebrities, Benny Benson. Benny was only thirteen years old when he entered a contest to design Alaska's state flag. He won the contest and the Jesse Lee Home had the honor of being the first place in the state to raise the new flag. Benson went on to live in the Aleutian Islands, eventually marrying and making his home in Kodiak, where he passed away at age fifty-eight.

While the children who lived in the Jesse Lee Home are always an interesting part of Alaskan stories, it's the children who died there that still make their presence known today. In 1964, one of the nation's worst earthquakes hit Alaska. Seward, being a coastal town, was hit especially hard, with a tsunami hitting the area and causing a section of the waterfront to slide right into Resurrection Bay. The Jesse Lee Home also suffered extensive damage, the worst of which was the deaths of over a dozen children. The school was nearly beyond repair and was moved to Anchorage where it became today's Alaska Children's Services. The old building, dilapidated and condemned, still sits empty at the edge of town.

Paranormal activity seems to abound on the grounds, with people exploring the area often hearing the sounds of children laughing... even though there are *no children* around. There have also been reports of:

† sounds of jump roping and feet running;

† little voices echoing in hallways;

† doors slam;

† winds blow through quiet rooms

Empty and condemned, yet somehow still full of life and laughter...as the *spirits* of the children who both lived and died there *still play* amongst the ruins.

~~~~~

Kenai/Soldotna

Kenai and Soldotna sit just ten miles apart from each other on the Kenai Peninsula. While Kenai is one of the first towns established on the peninsula, Soldotna was originally homesteaded by World War II veterans. Kenai's name comes from the Russian traders referring to its people as "Kenaitze" or "Kenai people," while Soldotna's name was taken from the nearby Soldotna creek, which was thought to have come from the Russian word meaning "soldier."

It was primarily a commercial fishing hub through the 1920s, with homesteading in the 1940s further developing the area. In 1957, oil was discovered at Swanson River, just twenty miles northeast of Kenai and Alaska's first major oil strike. This meant more people moving to Kenai and the surrounding vicinity, creating rapid population growth.

Referred to as the "twin cities," these small towns run independently yet are intertwined in both history and current times. They have an integrated economy and a strong tourist draw, with fishing, camping, and local shopping all part of life here. It seems like there are other things that are accepted as part of life here, however, including haunted places and ghosts.

†††††††††††

Bailey's Furniture Store

Located on the Kenai Spur Highway, Soldotna's Bailey's Furniture store was once a grocery store. The building was erected in the 1950s and has been owned and operated by Bailey's for the last ten to twelve years.

Back when it was still a grocery store, there was an attempted robbery. The shift manager was held at gunpoint and told to unlock the store's safe. As he was kneeling in front of the safe to open it, he was shot in the back of the head. The murder was never solved.

The store is thought to be haunted by the ghost of the murder victim, with furniture getting moved around or broken in the middle of the night and footsteps coming from above the upstairs office.

Manager John McDonald has been with Bailey's going on seven years.

"The ghost is almost a joke amongst those of use who work there," he says. "Whenever something comes up broken, we say the ghost must be mad."

McDonald qualifies this by adding, "I am kind of neutral about the supernatural. I certainly don't want to be disrespectful if there is anything to it, but I also don't want to sound like a crazy person!"

McDonald says that he is seldom in the store at night, working mostly during the day. He says that the ghost—if there is one—does not seem to be very active during the daylight hours.

"I do sometimes get a weird feeling," he says. "You know that feeling where it's like someone is watching you and the hairs stand up on the back of your neck? I've gotten that a lot there."

He states that while he has never had anything happen that has left him frightened, he has had a couple of odd things occur at the store.

"A couple years ago, we got a new alarm system," he says. "One of the switches had come loose on a door, and I had to go all the way around back to fix it and then come all the way around the front to re-set the alarm. There is a hallway between the buildings, and as I was walking by, I heard a jingling noise, like keys. I am one who always looks for the logical explanation of things, but I couldn't explain that sound."

McDonald is sometimes at the store in the early morning hours, resting between shifts as he maintains a second job as a snowplow driver.

"When I am in the office upstairs, I have sometimes heard odd noises coming from up above. When I go up to the storage area up there to investigate, there is nothing there," he says.

Other former employees have claimed that they too have heard noises above the office area, as well as finding furniture moved that should not have been disturbed. If the ghost is the murder victim, perhaps the only thing that will truly set him to rest is the conviction of his killer.

~~~~~

Homer

Homer sits on the shores of beautiful Kachemak Bay and is the southernmost town on the Alaska Highway system, hence its nickname, "the end of the road." Locals laughingly refer to Homer as a "quaint little drinking village with a fishing problem." The Homer Spit, as it's called, is a narrow 4.5-mile bar that runs into the bay from the downtown area and has a host of restaurants, shops, and beachfront.

The Alutiq people are thought to have camped here in early times. The town itself was named for Homer Pennock, a gold mining company promoter who arrived in Homer in 1896 and set up a camp for himself and his men. The town was also a big coal mining operation until World War II, and there are still tons of coal deposits in the area.

A popular spot for summer visitors, it is also haven to many local Alaskan artists, with galleries and shops tucked away in almost every corner, and has a certain flair that is undeniable. The population hovers at just under 4,000, with some of the more colorful year-round residents including authors, former Olympic athletes, musicians, and adventurers.

There are some other year-round residents in Homer, but they don't make the census count. There are endless stories about ghosts and apparitions, some perhaps fueled by the creativity and imagination of the artistically minded residents, some more difficult to explain. Of course, the older buildings hold the best stories, as the history behind them gives more credence to the tales themselves.

††††††††††††

Olson Lane Cabin

Located at the end of Homer's Driftwood Inn, the Olson Lane Cabin used to be a casket storage building and is now a private residence. While there have never been any substantiated reports of ghostly happenings, there have been some unusual things seen near and around the cabin.

One story says that one night in the cabin, an apparition that looked like an older woman appeared, standing in a corner of the room with her back to the residents. Other times, the woman has been seen standing outside the cabin, attempting to open the front door. The woman is wearing a long dress and has her hair up in a bun, and she has wire-framed glasses on.

There have also been footsteps, both inside the cabin and outside, and a group of men's voices can sometimes be heard late at night.

~~~~~

Salty Dawg Saloon

Homer's Salty Dawg Saloon is considered a landmark in the area and is a must-see on every tourist list. Erected in 1897, it was one of the first cabins built in Homer. It has been a post office, a railroad station, a grocery store, and a coal mining office, with a second building constructed in 1909 that operated as a schoolhouse and store over the years.

It was opened as the Salty Dawg Saloon in 1957, by Chuck Abbatt. After Alaska's 1964 earthquake, the structure was moved to where it stands today. It's currently owned by John Warren.

The saloon is an active part of Homer nightlife, and locals congregate there alongside the out-of-towners. It has a generally convivial atmosphere, and the stories that circulate tend to be mild, with any ghostly experiences falling more on the side of odd rather than frightening.

An old friend of mine, who seems to attract the paranormal, told me of a time he was at the saloon. "I was sitting at the bar, looking around at all the memorabilia that fills the place. Suddenly, I felt a hand on my shoulder. I thought it was the bartender, trying to get my attention. When I turned around, no one was there and the bartender was standing at the other end of the bar, talking to some patrons."

Other sources claim that there is a "friendly spirit" that lives there, who sometimes playfully knocks over glasses or scoots a chair into the walkway. Of course, some of the "friendly spirit" sightings may simply be a result of too many "friendly spirits" of the liquid variety, as employees of the saloon say they've never heard any ghosts there or experienced them.

Part Two

Interior Alaska

Chapter Six

Fairbanks

ike so many places in Alaska, gold was the defining factor that brought people to Fairbanks. With humble beginnings as a trading post in 1901, gold discovered in the nearby creeks in 1902 made Fairbanks a boomtown.

The trading post was started by Captain E. T. Barnette and was named "Fairbanks" in honor of Charles Fairbanks, a senator from Indiana who was greatly admired by a local judge. Barnette gave the town this name in exchange for help from the judge, James Wickersham, in building up the town. Wickersham aided Barnette by building his government offices in Fairbanks, and by late 1903, Fairbanks was an incorporated city. Barnette became the first mayor.

With the gold rush came the usual havoc, and the later influence of mining, the railroad and the eventual discovery of oil and the Trans-Alaska pipeline. All of these factors served to not only increase the growth of the city, but created an interesting mix of people. Those wishing to cash in on the weakness of others were quick to put up gaming halls, saloons and a "red light" district. As is the case with many parts of Alaska, that combination of gold, liquor and sheer desperation made for an interesting history, with many places holding onto that past via hauntings and other strange occurrences.

Since then, Fairbanks has continued to grow and is now the second largest city in Alaska. It has a population of just over 80,000 and is a popular tourist destination, full of activity and bustle. People enjoy exploring the history of the area, and some have seen a bit of history come to life, in ways they did not expect!

††††††††††††

Birch Hill Cemetery

Located off Steese Highway in Fairbanks, Birch Hill Cemetery is one of the oldest in the area. Gravestones here are often unreadable, with names faded and worn. The cemetery was taken over by the Fairbanks Funeral Home in 2007, and since that time there has been much strife over the use of the property. Originally designated for use as a cemetery only, there have been ongoing land disputes between the new owners and the Fairbanks Native Association over uses of the cemetery.

Like most cemeteries, Birch Hill has its share of ghost stories. There is a rumor of young girl in a white dress being seen here on occasion, wandering about the cemetery. Other visitors to the cemetery claim to hear voices and footsteps, and get a feeling of coldness when standing near certain graves.

Investigators from the group PEAK have said that their experiences there included obtaining some interesting photos of orbs...indicating that there is a definite presence there.

~~~~~

This is a mysterious photo taken during an investigation of the Birch Hill cemetery in Fairbanks. *Courtesy of PEAK Alaska.*

This photo is thought to contain an unusual orb, located to the left of the cross.
Courtesy of PEAK Alaska.

Chena Hot Springs Road (Mile 8-12)

Chena Hot Springs Road is a fifty-seven-mile paved road that goes east from Fairbanks. Traversing through the Chena River State Recreation area and terminating at Chena Hot Springs Resort, this is a very scenic and popular drive for tourists and locals alike.

A pair of prospectors known as the Swan brothers discovered Chena Hot Springs in 1905. One of the brothers apparently suffered from arthritis and, when they discovered the hot springs, they built a cabin and spent the summer there, resulting in his being cured. Soon people seeking the "magic" cure of the hot springs flocked to the area, and by 1915 it became an operating resort.

If you drive the road late at night, it becomes something more than just a beautiful drive. Reports of strange lights have been reported, specifically between miles eight through twelve. The lights have appeared as a headlight following passing cars, yet there is no vehicle there. The lights have been seen as both white lights and bright blue or orange lights, sometimes flying up in the air, sometimes skimming low along the ground.

~~~~~

Arctic Circle Hot Springs Resort

Located just over one hundred miles outside the city of Fairbanks is the Arctic Circle Hot Springs Resort. Originally utilized by the Athabascan Indians, local miners made use of the natural hot springs during the Gold Rush days.

Fairbanks resident Frank Leach homesteaded the property back in 1902, constructing a house and a lodge. Frank and his wife Emma ran the lodge until his death in 1955, with Emma continuing to run it alone until she passed away in 1974. The resort today consists of the lodge and a huge Olympic size swimming pool, which is fed by the natural hot springs. Always privately owned, it has been closed and up for sale.

Guests of the lodge have reported seeing strange things and hearing noises. Since most of the sightings have involved a female, it's thought that a woman, perhaps Emma Leach, haunts the lodge. There is a story that talks about an employee coming downstairs and seeing a woman wearing a fur coat, rummaging in the refrigerator. He claimed it was Mrs. Leach. Other employees have claimed to hear someone whistling in the kitchen area, as well as finding bedding mussed in various rooms that were recently made up.

The nearby cemetery only adds to the mystique of the lodge. Consisting of about thirty graves dating from the mid 1920s, many of them have fallen into disrepair, with dilapidated markers that sag into the ground and inscriptions faded into nothingness.

~~~~~

Chatanika Gold Mine

Chatanika is located twenty-eight miles north of Fairbanks on Steese Highway and is part of the Fairbanks-North Star Borough. Established as a mining settlement in 1904, it once was one of the richest areas for gold in the state. Between the 1920s and 1950s, over seventy million dollars in gold was mined there. The old gold dredge that was used to mine this gold still sits across the street from the Chatanika Lodge, a rustic trading post built in the 1930s that was turned into a modern Alaska roadhouse. Evidence of the old gold camp is still there, with the old abandoned hotel buildings still standing. There is other evidence there as well—evidence of the past making its way into the present.

Sources claim that in one of the abandoned buildings, the form of a young woman dressed in a white wedding gown runs across the hallway and vanishes into a wall. There have been other stories of ghost sightings, as well as voices, footsteps, and activity by angry poltergeists.

The folks who run the lodge say that many people who have visited the nearby gold mine say it's haunted.

The lodge owners also say that they sometimes think they have their own "friendly ghost" ... one who likes to move things around and create mischief.

Chapter Seven

Glennallen / Tok / Valdez

The area that includes the towns of Glennallen, Tok, and Valdez is full of history. The Ahtna Indians would come through in search of fish and game, eventually making homes and maintaining a population here even today. In 1899, the Army built a trail to carry supplies between Valdez and the town of Eagle, which eventually became Richardson Highway. Glennallen started as a camp for the workers who built Glenn Highway, which was constructed during World War II and completed in 1945. During the 1960s, the Tok Cutoff was built near the small community of Tok, tying in the other parts of the interior.

Nearby Valdez was originally named by Spanish Explorer Don Salvador Fidalgo, for naval officer, Antonio Valdes y Basan. As it was an ice-free port, it rapidly developed into an important freight hub, as Gold Rush fever brought in prospectors, who were disappointed to find that Valdez was not an easy access route to the gold fields. The town almost didn't make it through Alaska's 1964 earthquake, which created so much devastation that the original town site had to be abandoned and moved.

The area today remains a hub for those traveling from Canada through Alaska, and the Valdez port supports commercial fishing, oil exports, and tourism. The lingering spirits spoken of here are all that remain of the old days, as the towns are fully modernized although still retain their rustic feel.

†††††††††††

Mendeltna Creek Lodge

The Mendeltna Creek Lodge is located along Glenn Highway, thirty-five miles from the town of Glennallen and 153 miles from Anchorage. The area was originally used as a stopping point along the trails used by native Alaskans traveling from Lake Tyone to Tazlina Lake. The Gold Rush brought prospectors in the late 1800s, and currently retains its usage as a stopping point along the highway.

The lodge was constructed in 1940, with an addition built in 1950. It has had a succession of owners of varying character. A woman named Bonnie came to Alaska in the '50s after a stint in prison. Her mother bought her the lodge, perhaps as a means of getting her out of town and away from bad influences. Bonnie had a knack for finding trouble, however, and she and her boyfriend Eugene, who came to Alaska with her, soon found enough bad influences in Alaska to last them a lifetime. They set up the lodge as a chop-shop for stolen vehicles — current owner Mabel Wimmer says there are still a ton of junked cars in the back of the lodge, which she has slowly been removing as time and money allow. Their little business was quite successful, but that did not stop Bonnie and Eugene from fighting regularly. Theirs was a volatile and unpredictable relationship.

One day, Bonnie disappeared. Eugene told everyone she moved back to the "lower 48" to be with her family. He was anxious to sell the lodge and signed on the deed that he owned it. However, when the time for the actual sale came, it was discovered that he and Bonnie had never been married and his name was not on the property at all. Soon, suspicions arose about his involvement in Bonnie's disappearance, especially when her family back home reported that she had not returned there as Eugene had claimed.

Rumors, some spread by Eugene's own bragging, said that he actually had shot Bonnie with her own gun. He recruited two native boys to assist him in chopping up her body, which he disposed of by putting the flesh down the toilet and burning the bones in various brush piles around the property. He was investigated for the crime, but there was never enough evidence to prove he killed her. Eugene did eventually find his way back to jail via insurance fraud and the stolen vehicle/chop shop business.

Mabel Wimmer and her family have owned the lodge for six years. A self proclaimed skeptic of the paranormal, she says that she has had to admit that there have been some unusual happenings at the lodge.

"I have always been a skeptic," she says, "but I'm not so much anymore. There have been too many creepy things here, TOO many weird incidents!"

Wimmer says that the Alaska Paranormal Research Society has come to investigate the lodge a couple times—and the results indicate a definite presence at the lodge. "They found some voices on their tape recorders and had some areas of the lodge that seemed to have activity," she says.

So who is the ghost? Wimmer laughs when asked and says, "Everyone says it's Bonnie, the woman who was murdered by her boyfriend Eugene. Guests say they come into the main lodge to find chairs moved around and silverware messed up on the tables. Some have even said they've seen the shadow of a woman pass through the halls!"

One former employee said she could always smell pipe smoke in a certain area, even though smoking is no longer allowed in the lodge.

Wimmer says that some people have even claimed the ground in the Mendeltna area is haunted, the result of hundreds of people dying in the late 1950s during an Influenza outbreak. The riverbanks were also a prime burial ground for natives making their trek from the Anchorage area to the northern regions. People say the ground is "angry" and the creek is haunted.

While no longer a full-blown skeptic, Wimmer does tend to shrug off most of the stories behind the lodge. "How do I live here?" she repeats when asked the question, and answers simply, "Well it's home, you know. It's home."

~~~~~

McCarthy Lodge

The town of McCarthy started as a homestead and, with the arrival of the Alaska Railroad, became a big freight and passenger drop for Kennicott mine as well as nearby Shoshanna camp. McCarthy was a transit point for many of those seeking their fortune in Alaska, making it a popular place for prostitution and bootlegging. McCarthy is located in the Wrangell St. Elias Park, 130 miles from Glennallen off McCarthy Road. Wrangell St. Elias Park consists of thirteen million acres, one million of which are native and private lands.

McCarthy Lodge started as a cannery building in Katella, outside of Cordova. It was dismantled, shipped to McCarthy, and re-erected, where it became a photography studio and store. It's the oldest building in McCarthy, having been constructed before the town itself was even in existence. It was later renovated, along with the building next door, into a lodge.

Today, the lodge consists of a restaurant and saloon, with the building next door, Ma Johnson's, accommodating guests. Ma Johnson's is the only authentic historic hotel in the Wrangell St. Elias Park and is sometimes referred to as the "living museum." The hotel was built in 1923, owned and operated by the Johnson family as a boarding house.

From the 1940s until the early '70s, the town was mostly abandoned, although there were always a few local residents. Resurgence in local tourism helped re-establish the town, and it maintains a strong tourist trade with visitors flocking there every summer.

Neil Darish took over the lodge in 2001. He says, "I have never had anything happen to me that was unusual or even spooky. I have, however, had guests tell me some stories."

In room 2 of Ma Johnson's, there is a leaded glass mirror that is originally from one of the homes in Kennicott. Apparently guests have told Darish that they see a child or woman in the reflection of the mirror, and also hear voices in the hallway.

Darish says that he doesn't put too much stock into the stories. "I've never had anyone scared or hurt. There were a lot more stories before I took the property over, so maybe some of it was just folklore. There is nothing I would attribute to a ghost here. I don't believe in any of that myself."

~~~~~

Gakona Lodge

The Historic Gakona Lodge is located at mile "2" of the Tok Cutoff, just past Glennallen, Alaska. It's one of the only original remaining roadhouses in the area. Originally serving as a fish camp for the Ahtna Indians that inhabited the area, it was constructed as Doyles Roadhouse in 1904. In 1910 it became the main stop for the Orr Stage Company, as well as a regular resting spot for travelers. Today the lodge is still active and is listed on the National Register of Historic Places.

This is the Gakona Lodge...in which one can hear footsteps and voices when no one is around. *Courtesy of Valori Marshall*.

The lobby of Gakona Lodge...one of Alaska's original roadhouses. *Courtesy of Valori Marshall*.

There seems to be a regular resident at the lodge, with odd occurrences also happening in the older buildings. Doors opening and closing of their own volition, and voices and footsteps heard when no one else is around is not uncommon. Past guests have also reported tobacco smoke from an "invisible" pipe. Most of the activity takes place during the evening hours. No one sleeps in room 2, where it's reported to be cold and damp with a strange entity hanging out there.

These poltergeists may have moved on, however, as current owner Valori Marshall states matter-of-factly that they have lived at the lodge for over five years and have yet to experience anything out of the ordinary.

"We are certainly believers, as we lived in a home years ago that had a ghost," says Marshall. "People ask about the ghost and we are happy to show them the room that is supposed to have the most activity...but we have never witnessed anything. We did have the lodge blessed by our priest when we moved here, so maybe that accounts for the lack of activity!"

~~~~~

Devil's Mountain Lodge / Nabesna

I never knew growing up that I had a ghost story right in my own family. My grandparents came to Alaska back in the late 1950s, living in Anchorage and eventually starting their own guiding business in a small corner of the Wrangell St. Elias Mountains. Located at mile "42" off Nabesna Road, via the Tok Cutoff and the small town of Slana, Devil's Mountain Lodge is a remote hunting, fishing, and flight-seeing locale. Guests come from all over the world to explore the region and try for that trophy size sheep or moose. The lodge was started by my late grandfather, Bill "Wild Bill" Ellis, who became known as "King of the Supercub Pilots" and left the lodge behind as a family legacy. My grandmother, Lorene Ellis, currently owns it with my uncles, Kirk and Cole Ellis, running it.

The lodge is just a few miles from the original Nabesna gold mine, which was staked as a mining claim back in 1925 by Carl Whitham. Nabesna Road was built in the 1930s to facilitate the transport of ore to Valdez. The mine was shut down in 1945 because of World War II, but still produces small-scale mining and is privately owned today.

Devil's Mountain is a huge mountain that looms over the lodge, regal and majestic and a bit forbidding. I'd always assumed my family bestowed the name on it, but the story goes much deeper than that.

Devil's Mountain, located at Devil's Mountain Lodge, Nabesna Alaska and purported to be home to an evil spirit. This is my own family legacy of hauntings and the paranormal.
Photo by Jody Ellis-Knapp.

Back in the Gold Rush days, there were rumors of gold in the Wrangell St. Elias Mountains. A prospector decided to hike back and set up his claim there. Even today, Devil's Mountain is not an easily accessible area, and back then the roads were more trail than highway. But this prospector made his way there and staked his claim.

He holed up on the mountain, becoming reclusive and looking stranger and stranger every time he came down. He started talking of conversations he had with the Devil, spirits, and entities that apparently began to reside with him at his homestead. People started avoiding him, fearing his wild outbursts and even wilder appearance. Eventually, he stopped coming down from the mountain at all. When they went to look for him, they found him, dead. The cause of his death was never known.

Today, many people refuse to go near that mountain, saying its 'bad' and that the Devil truly lives there. Some of the native people in the area have said that no one should go there. My uncles, who are not superstitious in the least, say that there is a weird vibe to the area. Devil's Lake sits at the foot of the mountain. My uncle, Kirk Ellis, says the fish there are all deformed—trout never grows beyond a few inches and grayling with growths on their bodies. Of course, it makes sense that perhaps the lake is polluted with something from the mining days, but it still lends to the general air of mystery and trauma surrounding the area.

~~~~~

Mineral Creek Trail and the W. L. Smith Stamp Mill

Located in the Valdez area, Mineral Creek Trail is one of the more scenic places to visit. It can be accessed by car, hiking, or biking and gives a beautiful showcase of Alaska's splendor, alongside the history of the Gold Rush. Seven miles up Mineral Creek Canyon, at the end of the trail, sits the W. L. Smith Stamp Mill. Built in 1913, the mill was used to crush ore and mix gold with mercury. The mill is now state-owned and is a popular historic site.

There is a story of the Stamp Mill being haunted. People have said that when one stands behind the mill, the image of a man in a mining outfit suddenly appears in front of them. No one knows who the man is, if he died there, or if it's simply a trick of the light. Nevertheless, there seems to be some kind of energy associated with the mill—as there is with many old buildings. Other people have reported a feeling of being watched, or a sense of someone else having just been there when they visit.

Part Three

Southeast Alaska

Chapter Eight

Skagway

Stepping into the town of Skagway is a bit like stepping into a time machine. Rich in Gold Rush history, this small town is home to less than 1,000 year-round residents, with those numbers swelling into the tens of thousands each summer during tourist season. A popular port of call for cruise ships today, Skagway was originally a hunting ground for the Chilkoot and Chiklat Indians. In 1896, gold was discovered some six hundred miles from Skagway; and by 1897 Gold Rush fever had begun. Skagway had over 8,000 residents by 1898. Known as one of the roughest places in Alaska at one point, Skagway boasted over eighty saloons and many houses of "ill repute."

Skagway works hard to keep its history alive, reflected by the old-time style of the storefronts in its downtown area. While tourists flock there all summer, the underlying history of the Gold Rush days permeates every nook and cranny. Skagway's somewhat infamous past makes the ghost stories that surround many of its historic buildings quite believable. Alcohol flowing and gold rolling in meant high stakes and hot tempers. Perhaps some of the entities that have been known to hang around Skagway's old buildings are looking for just one more chance at the Gold Rush...one more opportunity to strike it rich.

†††††††††††

Golden North Hotel

Like any frontier town, Skagway has had its share of violent happenings, criminals, and tragic events. These events have left in their wake a smattering of paranormal presences, with perhaps the most famous being the activity seen at Skagway's Golden North Hotel.

Room 23 of the Golden North Hotel has been providing guests with a bit more than the average hotel stay for many years. Haunted by the presence of a ghost that employees have named "Mary," those who have stayed in the room have experienced images of a woman seen from their peripheral vision, as well as waking to choking sensations in the middle of the night. "Mary" is thought to be the ghost of a young woman who was waiting for her fiancée to return from gold prospecting. She died of pneumonia in the room before he could return...yet *she* still waits for him today.

Guests have also complained of a light in room 14. The light has been seen moving around the room at night. No one has been able to determine what the light might mean or what its presence might be.

Current owner Nancy Corrington says they inherited "Mary" when she and her husband bought the property back in 1997—and she believes Mary was real. She says:

"I think that the story of Mary is one of the longest living stories that came out of the Gold Rush. We did not try to add to or enhance her story for commercial purposes. In fact, we hesitated to even mention her because we had several personal events that led us to believe she did indeed reside in the hotel. As much as we tried to be realistic, we couldn't shake the smell of her perfume, the cold wind on the nape of our necks when there was no breeze apparent, faucets turning on by themselves, the closing of doors, and the movement of furniture from one place to another when the hotel was not occupied. Some people refute the legend of Mary, even people connected with the hotel. However, there have been multiple claims of ghosts that have grown exponentially with the number of tourists that now land in Skagway each summer. And why not? Everyone loves a good ghost story!"

~~~~~

Red Onion Saloon

The Red Onion Saloon, built in 1897, was originally the most exclusive and well-known bordello in the area. It was built by former Seattle resident, Peter Lawson, and operated as a saloon and brothel for roughly two years, serving drinks downstairs and offering the services of the ladies in a series of tiny rooms upstairs. The system used by the bartender to keep track of which ladies were "occupied" involved keeping ten dolls behind the bar. Each doll represented one of the working girls, and when she was with a customer, the doll was moved from a sitting position to lying on her back. Each room also had a hole in the floor with a tube that connected to the cash register. Money was sent from the room to the saloon so the bartender could track their earnings.

After the Gold Rush, the building was moved from the southeast corner of Sixth Avenue to Second Street and Broadway. It was shut down in 1916, but eventually re-opened and is currently owned and operated by J. Wrentmore. Today it's a national historic building and its checkered past is what helps bring clientele into the bar and restaurant.

It's inevitable that this kind of atmosphere would eventually bring about violence. The Red Onion's main resident ghost is named "Lydia" — she's thought to be a former prostitute who worked at the hotel and was murdered. According to Operations Manager Liz Lavoie, while guests have sometimes sent photos of strange anomalies, it's usually the employees who witness the paranormal activity.

"A recurring incident is the male employees feeling a 'shove' when they exit the brothel via the back staircase," she says, "and several of our 'madams' (tour guides) have had occurrences over the years. One of the more dramatic events was when our tour guide 'Lucy Longtime' was taking some guests through the brothel. She introduced them to our ghost, Lydia, and as she was doing so, a bed frame that we have hanging up on one of the walls lifted up from the wall and slammed down three times!"

Lavoie recounted another eerie occurrence involving a radio show that has people call in when they witness something paranormal. The DJ received a mocking phone call from someone who claimed to be inside the Red Onion, saying, "I'm calling from the Red Onion brothel, which is supposedly haunted..." and in the background you can hear a woman's voice say, "Who are you? Who are you?"

Lavoie says that the room considered the most active is the upstairs brothel museum. While she herself has never witnessed anything more dramatic than the occasional door opening or closing for no reason, she said there have definitely been times when she has felt she was not alone.

"When that happens," she says, "I just talk to Lydia soothingly... the same way I do the few times I've been hiking and seen a bear. 'Hi Lydia, it's me. Just going to get some extra quarters!'"

Lavoie, who has been with the Red Onion for eight years, came to Alaska as a college student for the summer and ended up as a permanent Skagway resident. "I don't consider myself a skeptic," she says. "I would say I've always been reservedly open to all realms of possibility, while not being over-eager, if that makes sense."

~~~~~

A sketch of the Red Onion Saloon by Jim Robb.
Photo courtesy of Liz Lavoie.

The bar at the Red Onion Saloon, where the good time girls used to hang out and some never left.
Photo by Sunday Ballew. Courtesy of Liz Lavoie.

The Red Onion employees get into the full swing of the saloon's history!
Photo by Andrew Cremata. Courtesy of Liz Lavoie.

The Mulvihill House

This private residence was built in 1904 and was occupied by the Mulvihill family from 1914 to 1949. Owner "Mul" Mulvihill was the chief dispatcher for the White Pass Railroad and often sent telegraphs from the house.

Those who have lived in the house since his death are sure that *he's* still there. Doors opening and closing by themselves is not unusual, nor are the sounds of a telegraph tapping and heavy footsteps going up and down the stairs.

Today, the house is included as part of a historical walking tour through Skagway. Stories of ghostly inhabitants have faded, so it's possible that the ghosts have moved on to the next plane, or maybe they have found peace and are satisfied with the way the current owners care for the house!

~~~~~

The White House

When it sat as an abandoned dwelling on the edge of town, the White house didn't even need any ghost stories to feel a bit scary. Originally a private home, it was used as a hospital during World War II, eventually evolving into a hotel, then a daycare center, then back to a private residence until it caught on fire and ended up burned and abandoned in 1988.

Those who spent time in the house prior to the fire reported entities such as a woman standing at the foot of a bed and the same entity apparently conversing with a child that was visiting the house. The ghost is thought to be the woman who ran the daycare center that once occupied the house. This "woman in white" has also been seen wandering the empty halls of the house.

The house was purchased and renovated in 1990 by Jan and John Tronrud, along with John's brother Ralph and his wife, Lori. After many weekends and summers spent re-building the damage from the fire, they opened as the White House Bed and Breakfast in 1997.

Says Jan, "I have seen stories in the past about the place being haunted, but I think that is just folklore that goes along with an old, once-abandoned building. It isn't haunted as far as I'm concerned, and the only spirit here would be the Holy Spirit."

~~~~~

The Chilkoot Trail

It's to be expected that a site as full of history as the famous Chilkoot Trail would have a few ghost stories attached to it. A thirty-three-mile hike that starts in Dyea, Alaska (just outside Skagway), it goes through the Coast Mountains and Chilkoot Pass and ends at Bennet, British Columbia. The trail was originally used by the Tlingit Indians as a trading route. The 1896 Klondike Gold Rush brought the "stampeders," or those rushing towards that dream of wealth, who began using the trail to make their way into the Klondike Territory.

Today the Chilkoot is a landmark and a very popular recreational trail. In an attempt to preserve the artifacts and natural beauty of the area, the National Park Service has placed very restrictive limits on the number of people allowed on the trail at any given time. There are campsites and plenty of other hikers to keep people company, a far cry from the death march it often was for the stampeders.

Many died along the trail in their quest for gold. Ill-prepared for the hardships of Alaska and the physical challenge of a thirty-three-mile hike, much of which was more of a climb than a hike, these prospectors sometimes didn't live long enough to realize their dreams. In 1898, there was a story of an avalanche that killed seventy stampeders on the Chilkoot Trail. Those who hike the trail today say that the essence of those stampeders, as well as other adventurers who died along the trail, still linger.

Stories of strange sights, odd noises, and inexplicable happenings are plentiful along the trail. Hikers say they have seen strange swinging lights in the distance of their campsites...the kind eerily similar to the swing of a lamp hanging on a backpack. Other tales of whispered voices and bizarre hammering sounds have been reported, with the most disturbing story involving someone hearing a voice say "go back" while they were climbing the Golden staircase, a very steep portion of the trail.

Those who died on the trail were most likely frustrated and in despair at being left out of the chance of finding riches in the mines of Alaska. A harsh country even now, Alaska back then must have been insurmountable for some of the city people who made their way to the Gold Rush. It isn't too shocking to consider the likelihood of disgruntled ghosts remaining on the trail, still trying to make their way to a Gold Rush long dead.

Chapter Nine

Juneau

laska's capital city is like most Alaskan towns—rife with history and a rather wild past. Juneau started out as a fish camp for the Tlingit Indians. In 1880, prospectors Joe Juneau and Richard Harris found gold at Gold Creek and staked a 160-acre town site on the beach. Soon after, the area was flooded with boatloads of prospectors headed for a strike at the Gastineau channel and Juneau, originally called Harrisburgh, evolved into a town.

Juneau became a hard rock mining center when the gold in the streams ran out, with two big mills being created, the Alaska-Juneau and the Alaska-Gastineau. Douglas Island became home to Juneau's Treadwell Gold Mining Company. Production in the mine was strong until a cave-in took place in 1918, flooding three of the mines and ending the mine's operations.

In 1906, Juneau was established as the state capital. But Juneau's natural inaccessibility—the town can only be reached via plane or ferry, and weather can be quite volatile—led to a measure to move the capital in 1954. This went on for many years, with measures to move the capital to Fairbanks, Anchorage, and Willow. All measures inevitably failed and Juneau remains the state capital today.

Home to over 31,000 year-round residents, tourism is the main industry in Juneau today. There are many historic buildings and visitors enjoy exploring both the old artifacts and taking part in the many activities. It is a popular summer cruise ship dock and, despite the large amounts of rainfall each summer, remains one of the top spots for visitors to Alaska.

There are several buildings and areas in Juneau that are said to be haunted or have some kind of paranormal activity. I've touched on the main places here that seem to have stories attached, although with Juneau's history, I am sure there are others.

†††††††††††

Alaskan Hotel

Juneau's Alaskan Hotel was built in 1913 and is now on the National Registry of Historic Places. It is Juneau's oldest operating hotel. Built by two brothers named McCloskey and a man named Jules B. Caro, the Alaskan Hotel allegedly got its beginnings as a house of ill repute. According to locals, the main ghost of the hotel is a woman who, legend has it, fell on hard times when her husband went gold mining and did not return. She became a prostitute, residing at the hotel. Her husband returned some weeks later and was so incensed to find her 'working' in the hotel, he murdered her. Another variation of that story is that the husband actually died while out mining, and the wife subsequently died of a broken heart in their hotel room, room 315.

Site manager Charles O'Connor has worked at the hotel for just over a year. He says that guests have approached him with several different stories and experiences—many having to do with room 315. "Typically, every March, which is supposedly the anniversary of this woman's death, we get people who stay in room 315 and come back to report strange occurrences."

Among the reports are sightings of people dressed in old fashioned clothing in the hallways, as well as unusual incidents in various rooms. One employee of the hotel reported a constant coldness in room 219, with no apparent reason for the chill.

O'Connor says that until 1956, "Ladies of Excitement," as they were referred to in those days, were legal. There was one lady in particular who was a resident of the hotel and had one man very interested in her. She did not return his interest and he killed her. She has been reported being seen in the hotel, wandering about in a long floral dress and large hat.

A newer and more perplexing ghost is the Indian princess. According to O'Connor, last year a hotel guest came running downstairs screaming and saying she'd seen a woman in white buckskin coming up the stairs towards her. The woman had looked the guest right in the eye...and then *disappeared*. Hotel staff dismissed the report until a fisherman staying there, a "regular guy" as O'Connor puts it, *saw* the same thing.

"What's weird is that from the description of the looks and the clothing, this ghost is a Sioux Indian Princess. I could see an Alaskan Native Indian Princess, but a Sioux?" says O'Connor.

Since then, other guests have reported sightings of this ghost. Says O'Connor, "It's easy to be skeptical, but over the years, when people tell the same story in the exact same way, you have to believe that something is going on."

††††††

C. Scott Fry was the manager of the hotel for twelve years. He initially went to Juneau to visit his parents in 1985, as they had just moved there. He liked it so much that he decided to stay, working first as a doorman at the bar in 1993, eventually moving to the hotel's front desk, and working his way up to manager.

Fry lived on the premises most of the time he worked there and was privy to some interesting *sights* over the years. He says there were two incidents that really stood out in my mind, one in room 321, the other in room 312:

"One involved a local character that used to run around town, a guy we called Buckwheat Buddha. He was an African American kid, mid 20s, and we figured he was homeless, but he always seemed to have money for food or a place to stay. You'd see him all over town, jogging out North Douglas Highway or washing on the side of the road in a small stream. He always looked like he had just crawled out from the woods, with twigs in his hair.

"One evening he showed up at the hotel, checking in to room 321, which happened to be on what we call the 'active' side of the hotel. Later that night, I received a complaint from one of the adjacent rooms of a disturbance coming from that room. I went upstairs to find out what the problem was, and when I entered the room, Buckwheat was standing in the middle of the bed, screaming obscenities and garbled nonsense at the ceiling. He held a bible in his hand and appeared to be reading from it, although I doubt any of what he was saying was coming from the bible. When I finally got him talked down, he told me that it was the spirits in the hotel doing all the yelling and that they were extremely ticked off. He checked out later that day."

*****

"It was the same situation, a woman checked in to the room and we later had guests calling down to complain about the noise. When I went to her room, the woman was screaming at the top of her lungs for 'Eagle Man.' She was laying on her bed with only her toes and shoulder blades touching—it looked like something right out of the *Exorcist*. She kept talking to someone in the room and it wasn't me! She ended up leaving the room that night with the ER techs, on a hospital gurney."

††††

Joshua Adams has been managing the hotel for the past five years, but has worked there in varying capacities for twelve years. His family has owned the hotel since 1977. Adams says his own ghost experiences fall more under sensing odd things than actual sightings.

"I've always been interested in reading auras," he says, "and the hotel has an aura all its own. There is an *energy* in this hotel, an energy that goes back to the Middle Ages."

Dismissing ghost hunting as a "superficial" endeavor, Adams nonetheless has seen his share of guests coming to explore the paranormal nuances of the hotel.

"People seem to either love it or hate it here," he says. "Historically, this hotel is one of the best examples of Victorian architecture you will ever see. But the shared bathrooms and antique atmosphere may not appeal to everyone."

Working in a hotel that has so much history inspired Joshua to write a book that gives a detailed accounting of the background of the hotel, prior guests and employees. The book, *The Life and Times of the Alaskan Hotel*, is for sale on the hotel website and at the hotel itself.

~~~~~

Mendenhall Valley Mine

Mendenhall Valley in Juneau is named for physicist Thomas Corwin Mendenhall. The valley was formed by the Mendenhall glacier and carries the main population of Juneau. It starts ten miles from downtown, ending ten miles west near Mendenhall Loop road.

Due to the history of gold mining in Juneau, the valley has many old mines scattered around different areas. There is one mine in particular, however, that seems to have some activity that has nothing to do with mining. The Alaska-Juneau mine, located about 1.5 miles outside of Juneau, contains the main mine, as well as several smaller ones. The mine itself was in operation until 1944, when it was closed due to being considered "nonessential" because of World War II. The mines onsite, while still visible, are rapidly returning to nature and there is a museum there that will show visitors some of the historic tools and artifacts of the era—for a fee.

Late in the day, however, there seems to be more to the mine than meets the eye. As the story goes, back when the mines were still in full operation, there were, as it happens in such a dangerous industry, several deaths. One man in particular was killed when a slide occurred with no warning and he was buried in it. Since then, rumors abound about a man—or group of men—who haunt the mines.

One local resident claims to have seen a man standing in front of one of the mine entrances, pickaxe in hand and staring angrily ahead. Another claim is that of several men seen working inside one of the mines, in an area that is caved in. Voices have been heard drifting across the area, and heavy footsteps, like boots, echoing through mine shafts. Activity seems sporadic at best, however, with some locals saying they have never heard of anything unusual at the mines, and other people saying there is something strange going on there. But it looks like the miners are continuing their work, looking for gold and ore and all the earthly pleasures they can no longer enjoy.

Chapter Ten

Ketchikan

Ketchikan is located more than two hundred miles south of Juneau. It has a history of mining and fishing, remaining an active fishing community today. It's named for the Tlingit word "kitsch-hin," which translates to "creek of the thundering wings of an eagle," and was used as a fish camp by native Tongass and Cape Fox Tlingits. In 1885, a man named Mike Martin purchased 160 acres from Chief Kyan and this became Ketchikan Township. With the first cannery going in during the year of 1886 and gold and copper discoveries following in the 1890s, Ketchikan grew quickly. With that growth, the expected unrest came too. Fights, thievery, moonshine, and showgirls were all part of Ketchikan's rich past.

Today the town has a population of 14,500. Often referred to as the "Salmon Capitol of the World," visitors come to Ketchikan from all over, primarily during the summer tourist season. Both the Alaska Ferry and cruise ships stop in at the town's port, and the town caters to the tourist trade quite a bit.

†††††††††††

Ketchikan High School

Ketchikan High School was originally built in what is now downtown Ketchikan in the 1940s. In 1946, a student fell to his death from a catwalk in the school. Apparently he haunts the school today, transferring over with the other students when a new school was built in 1954 and visible to both students and staff when one is standing on stage in the theater and looking up.

The high school today seems devoid of any spirits or ghosts, with throngs of teenagers doing what teenagers typically do. The student who supposedly haunts the place has not been officially reported by anyone, although I am sure it's a great scare tactic that seniors might use on incoming freshmen. Regardless, the entity that keeps watch at the school is thought to be a peaceful one, a student who never got to graduate and is stuck in high school forever. Kind of makes you wonder what he could have done wrong in this life to be left with such a fate!

~~~~~

Ketchikan Bayview Cemetery

Ketchikan Bayview Cemetery sits on the edge of town and contains the graves of some of the city's pioneers. The first burial at the cemetery took place in 1911 with some 5,000 people buried there since.

People have told me that there are ghosts haunting the cemetery, though locals are likely to scoff at the idea. A story surfaced of a woman's head seen floating above the road that leads to the cemetery.

No one is sure who the woman is, but there is a correlating story of a woman who was murdered by another woman in the nearby woods. The women were fighting over a man and one of them decided that the best way to keep her man was to get rid of the other woman. So she lured her to the woods by having someone deliver a note to the woman, leading her to believe it was from the man in question. When the woman went there, the other woman was waiting for her and took an ax to her, nearly decapitating her in the process.

Since that time, occasional reports have surfaced of the woman's head floating on the road to the cemetery. While no one seems to know for sure whether or not the story really happened, it certainly adds to the mystery that surrounds cemeteries all over the world.

Chapter Eleven

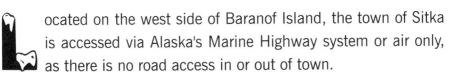

Sitka

ocated on the west side of Baranof Island, the town of Sitka is accessed via Alaska's Marine Highway system or air only, as there is no road access in or out of town.

The Russian influence in Sitka is evident everywhere you look. The site of the transfer of Alaska between Russia and the United States, it's the accepted site of Alaska's discovery by Russia in 1741, was headquarters for the Russian-American company that helped colonize the state, and also was the first location of the state capital.

The name Sitka comes from the Tlingit term "Shee Atika" or "People outside the Shee," which is the Tlingit name for Baranof Island. Sitka was originally established by Russian explorer Alexander Baranof as Fort Redoubt St. Archangel Michael at a site six miles north of the present-day town. Tlingit warriors destroyed the settlement just two years later, but Baranof would not be dissuaded. He left but eventually returned to re-stake a claim in the same area. The Tlingits fought hard, but were eventually defeated and had to retreat, leaving the claim to the Russian settlers.

Over time, Sitka went from a busy trading center to a quiet fishing village, until World War II brought a naval center and 30,000 military personnel. Today it's still a fishing hub, with a strong tourist leaning and is a major ferry stopover on the Marine Highway. There are over twenty-four attractions that are on the National Register of Historic Places. Amongst these historic places, it's inevitable that a ghost story or two will be told.

††††††††††††

Kiksaadi Club/Rookies Corner

A well-known bar in Sitka, the now defunct Rookies Sports Bar, was once known as the Kik, or Kiksaadi Club. One night, a woman left the bar while very inebriated, staggered into the road on what was a blind corner, and was hit by a man who had also been drinking and was driving. In her state, she did not realize what had happened and actually rose up after being run over, screaming and staggering around on the road until she eventually fell down again, dead.

Since that time, the woman is said to appear, staggering across the road, bleeding and silently screaming. She seems to hold a special place for those who choose to drink and drive, as she appears most often to them. Perhaps she intends to serve as a warning, or maybe locals just created the story to help keep the drunks off the street!

Part Four

The Far North

Chapter Twelve

Barrow

Barrow, Alaska is the northernmost settlement in both Alaska and the United States. Originally home to the Inupiat people, it was said to be discovered by French explorer Ernest Barreau, who was operating under orders from Russian Tsar Dezhnev. The colony became better known as Russian traders infiltrated and controlled the whale oil trade, eventually going from being called Barreau, to today's Barrow.

Oil field operations are the town's bread and butter these days, with a huge percentage of Barrow's 4,700 plus population working for North Slope Borough. While modern times have intruded on many of the traditions of the native people there, a subsistence lifestyle and many of the old ways still run strong through the community. Whaling is still a major event, usually occurring in mid-October, and many of the festivals and celebrations throughout the year are taken from old traditions.

There is an air of mystery in Barrow. This may have something to do with the sixty-five days of darkness that descends on the town each year, or just the way time has stood still in some places. The darkness and cold definitely contribute to the general air of inscrutability that seems to inhabit this northern village.

††††††††††††

Rogers-Post Site

An unusual claim to fame for the town of Barrow is that the celebrated Will Rogers, along with pilot Wiley Post, died in a plane crash here in 1935. Post had built a hybrid plane, with huge fuel tanks and a 550-horse power engine. Famous for making a trip around the world in eight days in his own plane, Post was interested in investigating the possibility of a mail and passenger route between Russia and the West Coast. His good friend Will Rogers decided to accompany him as he took his unusual plane up the coast.

They were trying to make it to Point Barrow just outside the town of Barrow when they got lost in bad weather and ended up landing a short distance away, at nearby Walakpa Bay. They took off again, trying to make it to Barrow before the weather worsened, and as they did, the plane stalled and landed in a river. Both were killed instantly.

Two monuments were eventually erected at the site of the crash, and the Barrow airport was named after them.

Claims have been made of strange noises heard around the crash area, and some have said that they have seen a shadow cross the sky in the shape of a small plane. A strange aura does linger over the site, with two larger than life people possibly leaving remnants of their spirits when their bodies perished.

~~~~~

The Ghost Ship

This story may or may not qualify as a true ghost story, as it reads more like a series of unfortunate events, but it does have all the elements of the strange and mysterious happenings that go along with ghostly tales, which makes it worth telling.

The *S.S. Baychimo* was a cargo steamer owned by the Hudson's Bay Company. In July of 1931, the ship left British Columbia, journeying on what was a regular route to Eskimo settlements around the Beaufort Sea, as part of the fur trade. As they started home in September, the weather turned and winter hit. Ice quickly permeated the sea, causing the ship to become locked in and unable to move. The ship was mired near Barrow, and the captain and crew camped there for two days, waiting for the ice to loosen. Surprisingly, it did loosen and the crew was able to motor on west, but only for a short period and then it became bogged down in ice again. Eventually Hudon's Bay Company retrieved most of the crew, leaving a few behind to wait out the rest of the winter and retrieve the ship and its cargo.

One night a huge storm hit the area, keeping the remaining crew in their shelters and unable to venture out for many days. When they did go out, they were shocked to find the ship gone. The captain thought it must have broken apart and would be found later, submerged under the ice. The crew decided to leave the area, but not long after, a native hunter said he had seen the ship, floating on its own, forty plus miles from the original site. They were able to find the ship and salvage the cargo, deciding that saving the ship was impossible.

For years afterward, the company received reports from Eskimo villages in the area that the ship had been sighted, some claiming to have boarded it and found it relatively intact. In 1933, claims were made that the ship was back in the original waters where it had initially become ice-bound. Some of the local natives attempted to board the boat, but just as they did so, a huge storm came up out of nowhere and forced them back. The next day, the ship was gone again.

The last report of a sighting of the ship was in 1969, in the Beaufort Sea near Point Barrow. Sailing thousands of miles up and down the icy coastline, occasionally mired in ice but never re-claimed by man, the ship may still be drifting today for all we know. Apparently the Alaska Government did start up a search project to see if the ship could be located, but to date, it remains a mystery.

Chapter Thirteen

Kotzebue

T he village of Kotzebue is located at the end of the Baldwin Peninsula in Northwest Alaska, thirty-three miles north of the Arctic Circle. It has a population of just over 3,000 people, seventy percent of which are Inupiat Eskimo. Archeological evidence indicates that the Inupiat people have lived in the region for at least 9,000 years. It has historically served as a supply center and trading post, as well as a gathering place for people all around the area. Natives know Kotzebue as "Qikiktagruk," which translates to "almost an island" and notes that the town is on the end of a narrow spit on the Peninsula. The town name was eventually changed to Kotzebue after the Kotzebue Sound. Today it still serves as a transfer point between ocean and inland shipping and the regions main air transport center.

†††††††††††

Nullagvik Hotel

Owned and operated by the NANA Regional Corporation, this hotel is a popular stopover for visitors to the area. Clean and modern, you wouldn't think it had a haunted history, but it does.

Some people claim that the apparition of an old man haunts the offices that were once part of the hotel. No one knows who he is or what the history might be that brought him to the hotel, but several have said they have seen him, walking the down the hall with his back to the person. When the person calls out to him, he vanishes.

~~~~~

Frank Ferguson Building

The Frank Ferguson Building, named in honor of Senator Frank Ferguson, who was known for his pioneering efforts in the community, houses some of the offices for the Maniilaq Association, which provides health and assistance to rural Alaska residents.

For years, people have claimed that the building is haunted, with some refusing to even enter it. There is an old legend that the building was erected at the site of what was a fierce battle between two warring Inupiaq tribes. The residue of the bloodshed at that site has left behind the wandering spirits of those who died. There have been apparitions seen both inside and outside the building, as well as running footsteps heard near the building late at night.

Chapter Fourteen

Nome

The city of Nome was established on the south coast of the Seward Peninsula, along the Bering Sea. Already occupied by native Alaskans for thousands of years, gold was discovered at nearby Anvil Creek during the Klondike Gold Rush and it quickly grew into a town of over 20,000 people. Originally called "Anvil City," the name was officially changed to "Nome" when the post office kept disputing the name because they thought it was too close to the name of another nearby village, Anvik. After much dissent, the town agreed to the name of "Nome." Unfortunately, Nome doesn't come from the name of a famous explorer or from Alaska native languages, but a spelling error. In the 1850s a British officer noted on a map of the area an unnamed point, writing "name?" next to it. Someone transcribing the map misunderstood what he wrote, putting down "Nome."

One of the things Nome is most known for is being the terminus of "The Last Great Race," Alaska's Iditarod. The first official Iditarod race was held in 1973, along the historic Iditarod trail, used for centuries by Inupiaq and Athabascan Indians and later by miners on their hunt for gold. The most famous mushing event in relation to the trail is the 1925 serum run to Nome, in which there was an Influenza outbreak that threatened the lives of many people in Nome. Twenty mushers and more than one hundred dogs assisted in getting the serum the 674 miles from Nenana to Nome. That history remains a big part of the Iditarod race, and during the Iditarod, Nome becomes a busy tourist destination.

Today Nome is a commercial hub for the entire region, as well as a popular tour stop for visitors. Roughly 2,000 year-round residents live within the city, with many more on the outlying areas. It's an interesting mix of the old, traditional native ways and contemporary times, with snow machines a modern mode of transport yet dog sledding still a big pastime. The stories here tend to be eclectic too, a combination of old legends and more recent ghost tales. There are some interesting stories attached to some of the places in this arctic region...as they are believed to be occupied by something more than the usual bear or caribou.

††††††††††††

Pilgrim Hot Springs

Located at the end of sixty miles of rough road outside Nome sits the site of Pilgrim Hot Springs. It was set up as a Catholic mission and children's home in the mid 1900s after one of the more serious Influenza outbreaks that killed many people, leaving children orphans. It operated as such until the early 1940s. The chapel for the mission, Our Lady of Lourdes, still stands. Before that, it was supposedly a resort that was built during the Gold Rush, with a saloon and dance hall, along with the natural hot springs.

One local describes the place as "beautiful but creepy as hell," and says that she has heard several stories over the years of the area being haunted. Voices and other strange noises have been heard there, as well as there being just a general feeling of discomfort. The small outbuildings that housed the children are supposed to have a ghostly presence that can occasionally be seen as a fleeting shadow from the corner of a person's eye. Locals still enjoy going out to the hot springs, which has a large tub with a wooden frame built around it, and many say that the only scary thing they've encountered out there is the occasional wandering bear.

~~~~~

The "Last Train to Nowhere"

Standing on a strip of tundra, literally in the middle of nothing and nowhere, stand three locomotives from the 1880s. A wild plan to create rail service in and out of the Nome area during the Gold Rush left the town with thirty-five miles of track and three trains, all bound to go exactly no place at all—where does one go on the tundra with thirty-five miles of train track anyway?

The place is said to have an "eerie silence" and lingering there is likely to bring about strange thoughts and odd feelings. While no one has claimed to see an actual spirit, the remnants of the Gold Rush—and all the despair that went with it—seem very strong here. Some say that the ghosts of the miners remain here, still looking for gold; they claim to have felt a sudden chill when standing near the trains, or having a feeling of being watched when no one is there.

~~~~~

The Handyman

There is a story of an unnamed apartment building in Nome in which residents were complaining of a man trying to break in. They called the chief of police. He responded and could not find any signs of breaking and entering, although the residents had clear descriptions of what the man looked like. He went back to the station, looking over old mug shots to see if he could find someone who matched their descriptions. Eventually, he came back to the apartment building with a photo of a man to show the residents. They all agreed that this was the man in question. Unfortunately, the man they were describing had died at the apartment complex years earlier after falling off a piece of scaffolding he was standing on while doing some repairs to the building.

Part Five

Alaskan Folklore

While the Gold Rush and the early statehood years may be the most commonly discussed part of Alaska's past, there are also quieter legends that go much deeper than the relatively few years Alaska has been part of the United States.

Alaska's native people were here long before the prospectors. They have their own stories to tell about the history of Alaska, but this is a more difficult realm of information to access. Legends tend to be kept within the tribes and within families, with only remnants of information leaking out.

By far the most unsettling stories are those of strange creatures walking among us. Ranging from a 'Bigfoot' type creature that Alaska natives refer to as the "Big People" or "Hairy People" to smaller creatures known as Ircenrraat or "Little People," the far reaches of Alaska seem to have more than the standard bears or caribou living in the area.

††††††††††††

Ircenrraat/Little People

Known by the Yup'ik Indians as the "little people," the Ircenrraat (irr-chin-hhak), or Innukin, have been an active part of Alaska Native legends and history for centuries. Unsettling stories abound in Alaskan folklore, some so authentic and real that they seem to transcend the concept of folklore and move into a more concrete reality. The Ircenrraat have been blamed for getting people lost, frightening people and even abducting them. The people who claim to have seen the Ircenrraat are not just village storytellers keeping the tales alive, but residents who are considered reliable and sensible people.

Not long ago, an email surfaced in rural Alaska that became the topic of an article in the *Anchorage Daily News*. It discussed a local hunter who found a small boy alone and disoriented in the forest. Thinking he had gotten separated from another hunting party, the hunter asked the boy who he was with and what he was doing. The boy kept saying, "I don't know," and started crying. The hunter brought the boy back home with him. (The boy later told a story of being held captive by a group of little people. He was disoriented and seemed to have lost some time.)

Kristin Osborne of Mystery Alaska Research Society recounts a tale she heard of a woman in one of the villages who had gotten her snow machine stuck on a lake. The trail was very clearly marked with wooden stakes, so she was not overly concerned about making her way home on foot. She left her snow machine behind and set out. As she walked, she would look down at her feet occasionally. When she looked back up, it seemed like the trail markers had been moved. Eventually she realized that the markers were indeed moving, as she witnessed one go up and slide over. Having heard the stories, she was sure it was the Little People, trying to divert her off the path and get her lost.

Many stories of people disappearing, people who lived in the remote parts of Alaska and were avid outdoorsmen, always abound and the Little People always seem to be mentioned. They are a mischievous, sometimes malicious group who thrive on creating havoc, and who appear to have survived the influx of modern times. For many Alaskans they are far more than mere legends.

~~~~~

The Hairy Men

As with everything else Alaskan, the North Country's Bigfoot legends are above and beyond bigger and better, than any other North American tale.

Commonly known as the "Hairy Men" or the "Arulataq," Alaska's Bigfoot is said to be at least ten feet tall, with long arms and a loud, bellowing cry. Acting mainly under cover of night, the creature is said to be fond of raiding campsites, stealing fish from fishermen and has been blamed for the unexplained disappearances of both pets and humans.

While some may argue that Bigfoot is a shy, retiring creature, Alaska's Hairy Men seem different. Says Kristin Osborne of the Mystery Alaska Paranormal group, "I've never heard any positive story about the Hairy Men. It's always something scary, like them taking someone away." Osborne, who has spent time in many Native Alaskan villages, has heard stories of the Hairy Men throughout several areas.

One local Alaskan recalls an event that happened on the beaches of Cordova, told to her when she was a child. "My mom and a friend were walking on the beach, late at night. From the corner of her eye, my mom suddenly caught a glimpse of something running up behind them. She said it was very big and shaggy, walking upright on two feet but also loping low to the ground. As she turned, it veered into the nearby woods."

Another person said that he spent one winter living in a cabin in a remote part of Interior Alaska. It was night and he had been outside chopping firewood, some distance away from his cabin. As he started back towards the cabin, he saw a large shaggy figure standing at the window of his cabin, looking in. He stopped and waited, too afraid to approach. Eventually the figure wandered off the other way, and the man was able to go back to his cabin. He never felt completely at ease after that, however, and soon left the cabin and went back to town.

There is a book, published privately back in 1953, titled *The Strangest Story Ever Told*. The book spans twenty-five years of early Alaskan history, beginning in 1900. The book tells the tale of Charlie, a man who took a trip from Wrangell to Thomas Bay in search of gold. Gone from his friends for over a month, he suddenly reappeared in Wrangell one day, a strangely different person than he was before, with no possessions in hand but his canoe and a chunk of quartz. He eventually tells his friends that he wants to get on the next boat to Seattle, never wanting to see Alaska again. Apparently, while on his quest, he climbed a tree to get his bearings and saw, to his terror, a large group of "the most hideous creatures" racing up the ridge towards him. Describing them as "neither man nor monkey, yet looking like both" and "bodies covered with long coarse hair," Charlie claims he was chased by them and nearly caught. He did not recall making it to his canoe, but woke on the bottom of his canoe, drifting between Thomas Bay and Sukhoi Island. He did leave Alaska and was never heard from again.

The Athabascan people speak of the "Na'in" or brushman, who would sometimes kidnap people. The Na'in were originally said to have been men who were shunned from the tribe for various infractions of their laws. Lonely for companionship, they would sometimes kidnap women while they slept. Yet the powers of the Na'in seemed to exceed that of ordinary men. The legends include tales of the Na'in having mind control powers, with the ability to lure people to sleep so they can abduct them.

Whether it's called the Hairy Man, the Na'in, Bigfoot, or Sasquatch, the descriptions and stories seem to consistently resurface and in different regions of Alaska. Add in all the stories of sightings of similar creatures throughout Canada and the Pacific Northwest, it seems like there may very well be something to the tales.

~~~~~

Long Tail People

No one speaks much of the Long Tail people. My uncle told me a few stories, but said that if you ask a Native Alaskan about them, they are reluctant to speak of it. The stories seem to originate in the Copper River area, but no one seems to know from where exactly. There is a bad feeling associated with this creature. Some believe that talking too much about an entity or creature will invite it into your world, and from the description of the Long Tails, no one wants them coming to dinner.

The Long Tail people live under the banks of rivers, in the mud. They are ugly creatures with long monkey-like tails and have a light coating of hair, somewhat like a primate, but with a base human intelligence and their own societal structure. They do not show themselves often, only when hunger drives them from their refuge. They don't feed on animals or berries, however. Their meal of choice is of the human variety.

The legends say that the Long Tails have been known to steal small children from camps and eat them. There have been stories of people going hunting or out walking in the woods—people who knew the area well—disappearing along the riverbanks. There are some who will avoid the riverbanks of certain places during the twilight hours, as that is when the Long Tails seem to be most active.

There is some question as to whether or not the Long Tail people may be the same entity as what are called "Glacier Devils," reptilian looking creatures that are said to reside around some of Alaska's remote glaciers. The Glacier Devils are also known for their penchant for human flesh, so it's possible that the stories of the Long Tail people are a derivative of the legends of the Glacier Devils.

One man tells the story of a hike he took on one of Alaska's glaciers in a remote area. As he was walking across a section of the glacier, he saw movement in the hills nearby. Thinking it might be sheep, he took out his binoculars and tried to get a better look. He saw what looked to be a dark creature standing on two feet and looking right back at him. While his logical mind told him it was just a trick of the light, a reflection of the glacier ice, or his own mind playing tricks on him when he was tired, he quickly turned around and went back the way he came.

~~~~~

Thunderbirds

The legend of the Thunderbird is one that encompasses many parts of the United States, not just Alaska. This ancient legend has been part of Native American culture for many years, existent in various forms throughout many different tribes and regions. Native tribes such as the Ojibwa, Lakota, and Sioux all have stories associated with the Thunderbird, and Alaska's native people create beautiful totem poles that depict the Thunderbird alongside other mystical creatures.

A bird with enormous size and strength, Thunderbirds get their name from the idea that their wing span is so large, when they flap them it actually creates the sound of thunder. Some of the traditional stories state that it has a human face; some call it a deity and some see it as a supernatural being. Haida tradition shows Thunderbirds with a human face on their belly and their stories talk about Thunderbirds hunting for whales far out at sea.

It's easy to dismiss the stories as folklore, yet there have been various reports over the years of people actually seeing giant bird-like creatures in the skies of North America. In the late 1940s, a family in the Midwest apparently reported that they saw a monster bird that was "bigger than an airplane" flying overhead. Several reports came through in different parts of the region on the very same day of similar sightings.

In 2001, reports of Thunderbird sightings surfaced again, with people saying they had seen a bird the size of a small plane flying overhead in Pennsylvania. Other sightings were reported during that same time period, with one person describing the bird as having a wingspan of over fifteen feet and a body almost five feet in length.

Alaska has had its own Thunderbird sightings over the years, the most well known occurring in 2002. A man in Togiak, just west of the village of Manokotak, was working outside when he saw what he initially thought was a small plane flying towards him. As it banked, he realized it was not a plane after all, but some kind of huge winged creature. Later that week, a pilot flying a group into Manoktotak looked out the window of his plane and saw a huge bird about a thousand feet from his plane. He estimated the wingspan of the bird to be roughly fourteen feet in length, or the same as a Cessna.

There is some speculation as to whether or not Thunderbirds are actually some surviving species of pterodactyl, as depictions of the bird seem to most closely resemble this ancient reptile. Regardless, many people in Alaska believe that some version of this bird does exist. Many of the paranormal investigation groups around Alaska have shown interest in the Thunderbird, believing that there is definitely something to the story.

While it may not have the magical powers described in ancient legends, there does always seem to be a grain of truth somehow attached to these old stories, and the many Thunderbirds depicted in native artwork and tales seem to give credence that there is some kind of bird out there that surpasses a bald eagle in size.

Part Six

The Investigators

he concept of ghost hunting has never been more popular than it is today. With several regular television shows on various networks, books, video guides, seminars, and even Ghost Hunting certification courses available, it seems that everyone has jumped on the bandwagon of exploring the paranormal.

The term "ghost hunter" is inaccurate and highly "Hollywood-ized." None of these investigators set out to hunt or capture ghosts, as that would be impossible. Most prefer the term "paranormal investigator," as they are seeking out information and exploring unusual occurrences. Not all of what they find can even be classified as ghosts or spirits, and "Paranormal" better encompasses the realm of what they do. Many consider themselves researchers in the name of science, studying things that do not seem plausible and looking for answers.

Ghost stories do more than just give us nightmares or a thrill of adventure. Sometimes the history behind the stories is so interesting and so unusual, it inspires people to go beyond the mere telling of tales and actually start looking for proof of paranormal activity. We are all obviously looking for answers in this world, trying to make sense out of things that cannot be explained, or hoping for some inkling of what might be on the other side of life.

Whether from a personal experience that left them a believer, or a slew of stories that seem to ring true, there are those out there who research and investigate the possibility of the paranormal and the unexplainable. There are several groups of paranormal researchers in Alaska, some more serious than others. Some of the groups seem to be in it for the mere idea of "ghost hunting," yet others are dedicated towards trying to help people who are in the midst of a paranormal event in their home or business.

This section profiles some of the more well-known groups around Alaska, those who have investigated and gathered data from many of the haunted locales in this book and who truly believe that each story is worth checking out.

††††††††††††

Mystery Alaska Research Society

When Kristin Osborne moved into a tiny cabin in Fairbanks, Alaska, she was told that there had been some unusual incidents there. She laughed it off and moved in anyway. Soon she was hearing noises, finding lamps and other items unplugged when she left them plugged in, and having odd electrical problems. A "skeptical believer," she started thinking there was something definitely wrong with that old cabin. Kristin had a roommate move in and warned him that she'd seen some strange things. The roommate was friends with Steve Osborne, who was woken up late one night by him pounding on his front door, scared because he had seen "something" at the cabin. Steve went over to check it out, met Kristin and the two hit it off. Their romance went hand-in-hand with a desire to investigate the cabin, which led to a continuing interest in the paranormal.

In 2007, Steve and Kristin got a few other people together and formed Mystery Alaska Research Society (MARS). "Oh, it's a definite play on words," laughs Steve. "You know, Mars, like 'out there'?" But the things they have found in their investigations are no laughing matter.

One of their first investigations was the Anchorage Historic Hotel. They set up in the hallway upstairs and two of the rooms, one being the infamous room 215. Says Kristin, "It was during Fur Rendezvous and when we were setting up, we could hear two women next door, drawers slamming, water running, etc. I was hoping they were getting ready to go out because I was concerned that the noise would interfere with the investigation. Sure enough, the noise eventually stopped. I later found out that the room next door to us was actually unoccupied that night."

Steve Osborne says the most interesting part of the investigation is what the team calls "the camera incident."

"We had set up two cameras on tripods at each end of the upstairs hallway," he says. "Kristin decided to secure the cameras to the tripods with electrical tape, as she was concerned that someone might accidentally knock one of the tripods over and damage a camera. The cameras were facing each other so we could record all potential activity in the hallway. That night, one of the cameras can be seen, over a ten-minute period, slowing ripping away from the tripod. When we looked at it later, the tape had been noticeably torn away, as if by human hands."

The Mystery Alaska crew says that so far, the most exciting investigation they have conducted was at the Birchwood Saloon. They had been there twice already and were planning a third trip. I was lucky enough to be asked along.

We arrived at the saloon at 5:45 a.m. on the morning of November 1, just one day after Halloween. The crew, in addition to Steve and Kristin, consisted of Ricker Thayer, their lead investigator and electronics genius, as well as newest member Janet Taylor, a writer who has been investigating the paranormal for many years. Janet started out investigating old homes in New Orleans, and continued her interest when she moved to Alaska thirteen years ago. They began setting up their equipment, which consisted of a DVR with infra-red, various recording devices in different rooms, and digital cameras. They also have a state of the art video system that includes a four-screen monitor that allows them to track activity in any room they have equipped with a camera. They carry an EMF (Electro Magnetic Field) reader and a similar device known as a K2. Both gauge electro-magnetic fields and changes in the area.

Cameras were set up in the freezer, the storage areas, and the saloon's old and now defunct dining room. While setting up, Kristen and Steve talked about some of their findings during their last investigation.

"The last time we were here," says Steve, "I could feel the heaviness in certain rooms. This trip already feels different—it's more reserved, I feel a holding back."

Their video footage of their last visit to the saloon included an image of someone walking through the double doors that lead to the kitchen. "You can see the outline of a person very clearly," says Kristen, "and see the doors swing." Both Steve and Kristen said that the photos and audio recordings were also very interesting—one photo depicted a big vortex in the back room, and the audio recordings had voices trying to interject into the investigators conversations.

The investigation itself yielded no surprises or sightings for me, but Kristen said that until she had a chance to review the audio and video fully, they could not be sure that nothing happened. "It's usually after the fact that you see and hear stuff that is unusual," she said.

~~~~~

IOPIA (Investigators of Paranormal in Alaska)

Neelie Lythgoe and her friend and partner Tony Hernandez both grew up in Alaska. They went to school here and were interested in the paranormal long before it was the popular thing to do. As children, they talked about someday forming some kind of investigative group.

Today, they are the founders and primary members of IOPIA (Investigators of Paranormal in Alaska). The group has been in operation for fifteen years and is considered a highly respected authority on the subject of the paranormal. Says Lythgoe, "Not too many other groups have done this as long as we have—they usually don't last that long—but it's so much more than just a job to us. There is always so much to learn and do."

Neelie's interest in the paranormal started in childhood. "I grew up in a haunted house," she says matter-of-factly. "So did Tony. When we were kids, we would talk about it. When we were about thirteen years old, we decided that someday we had to have our own investigation group, and eventually we did."

Lythgoe states that she receives daily requests from people seeking help or information. "We are running about six investigations behind right now," she says. "People contact us and we try to help everyone. We take the worst case scenario first, where people cannot sleep at night or there are serious things happening."

One incident that involved serious things happening was at a private home in Sterling. According to Lythgoe, a priest had already been to the house and refused to return. The IOPIA group, at the request of the homeowner, decided to see what they could find out. Armed with their research equipment, they made the drive to Sterling and the house in question.

"This was a house in which beds and tables were levitating," she says. "A window shattered for no reason, the owner felt they were in real danger. During our investigation, one of the most frightening incidents was when a ball of light, roughly three feet in diameter, came through a window and straight towards one of us. I was using a camera that has a capacity sixteen times brighter than infrared, which means I can often see things that the others cannot. When this light came in, the other members started saying, 'Do you see that light? Do you see it?' and I was shocked that it was visible to the naked eye. I tried to reach out and touch it and it flew out the window." The group also witnessed beaded curtains in several doorways moving wildly, though no one was there, and a moment where something rushed down the hallway towards them.

Lythgoe says that at that house, they also got EVPs (electronic voice phenomena) off their tape recorders of a man's voice saying very threatening things. "We went back several times over the years," she says. "Eventually things settled down. This was something that most would consider demonic. It was what I would call a very physical house. In fact, when we showed up at the place, the owners had dug up almost the entire front yard, looking for a dead body or murder victim. That experience was the only time I saw Tony almost run out on me, and he is not easily frightened." The group was able to obtain some very believable apparition photos from the house.

Lythgoe says that she isn't sure why things calmed down after they visited the house, but speculates that perhaps the entity became frustrated because they did not run and did not appear frightened of it. "The person who is the most fearful is the one who is affected the most," she says, "and when you aren't getting that reaction, I think even for spirits it loses its luster."

IOPIA has investigated many different haunted places over the years, including Motherlode Lodge outside Palmer. "It can be difficult to obtain formal permission from some of the places, especially if they are closed down or government owned," Lythgoe says. "One of the first apparition photographs I ever got was at the Jesse Lee Home in Seward, when I was just there exploring. It has since been closed up and we have not been able to get permission to go there and actually investigate the stories behind it."

Various devices are used in the investigations. "We have a lot of equipment," says Lythgoe. "We have video cameras, both digital and tape. We have audio equipment, mostly digital because that produces the best results. We have EMF readers although I prefer not to use them, and we use thermometers to record sudden drops in room temperature."

There are four core members of the group. In addition to Lythgoe and Hernandez, two other members, Leah, a researcher in Fairbanks, and Patch, a senior member who works in communications and does much of their electronic work.

Lythgoe states that she is careful about who joins the group. "I don't let anyone join us unless they are over twenty-one. I cannot be liable for a teenager getting hurt and this kind of stuff can really mess with your mind and psyche," she adds. "It can be dangerous. It's more of a serious thing for Tony and me, rather than just doing it for fun."

Lythgoe takes her research and investigations beyond just basic "ghost hunting." She says, "There is much more to it than what you see on television. You have to know something about physics and science and about photography. Even about psychology! We have to talk to people who are distressed, who are in an emotional state, and dealing with something they may have never dealt with before. You have to know how to talk to people, how to help them get through this."

When asked about upcoming investigations for IOPIA, Neelie says that while she cannot be too specific, she does have some private investigations coming up soon. "There was an accident several years ago in Fairbanks," she says. "A man was hit by a car and killed. The death was ruled an accident. Not long ago, the man's brother contacted us. He said his brother had been appearing to him, saying he was murdered."

Lythgoe says the group also gets involved in investigating unsolved murder cases, researching evidence and employing local Alaskan psychics for their insight. "We use only Alaskan people in our investigations," she says. "That is very important to me."

The group is working on compiling their research on the paranormal into a book. "We try to help people," says Lythgoe. "We try to make this a better place."

~~~~~

Alaska Paranormal Research

Alaska Paranormal Research was founded in June 2006. Originally started by Deana Beard, Doug Aaron came into the group shortly thereafter and Janet Andrews joined the following month.

Doug Aaron says he became interested in joining a paranormal investigation group after a negative experience with the paranormal.

"Without going into detail, I had something happen to me years ago in relation to the paranormal. It was something I could not logically explain, and it made me remember a lot of things that had happened to me as a child. When I really started thinking about it, I realized that a lot of the things that had happened to me when I was young were related to paranormal occurrences."

Aaron said that he spent time as a child in a relative's house that was built around the turn of the century, and for many years he and his siblings had nightmares about the attic of that house. No one in his family would ever discuss what might have happened in that attic, but it left him wondering what could still be there that would cause such nightmares.

"I wanted to learn more and wanted to join a group," he says, "but a lot of groups didn't want me since I didn't have experience in tracking the paranormal. I am originally from Arizona and I always wanted to move to Alaska. I knew when I moved here I would never want to leave, which has been true so far! Once I moved here, I decided that I really wanted to get involved in investigating. I went online to see about joining a group. Deana had posted something on the (website) Craigslist about starting a group and we started talking. We ended up deciding to just start our own group."

The group is still a fairly young one, and they are still, according to Aaron, "working the kinks out" when it comes to their organization.

"It's hard because this is a volunteer situation. It can be difficult to keep people around on a regular basis."

They have investigated some private homes, as well as Eagle River's Birchwood Saloon. "We've actually gone back to the saloon a couple times," says Aaron. "We did have some interesting things happen there. Once when we were there, we distinctly heard someone walking around on the roof. When a member of the team checked out the roof, no one was there. We also had a brand new camera battery die when we were attempting to take pictures, and we had to re-record some of our interviews there as the recorder showed that it was recording, but when we went to play the tapes back, they were blank."

Aaron says the Birchwood Saloon is where one of the group's more unsettling events occurred.

"I was using a digital recorder," he says, "and I was asking some random questions around the room, such as 'who are you?' I asked the question, 'do you like it here,' and later when we played the recording back, you could hear a woman's voice saying very strongly, 'No!' That was really uncomfortable to me, the whole idea of being trapped somewhere you don't want to be after death!"

They were also able to come away from Birchwood saloon with a photo that shows the outline of a man sitting in a chair, dressed in what looks to be pilot's clothing. This has become a somewhat famous photo around the investigative circuit, and other groups have gotten similar images.

The group has also investigated some private homes, which must remain nameless due to client privacy. "I had an experience with one that involved some strange growling sounds coming back on a tape recording," says Aaron. "That is kind of disturbing because you don't know what it is. When you hear a human voice, you at least know it's a person. When you hear growling, you can't be sure what it is you are hearing."

The group is always open to other people joining or participating in their activities. "We basically started out wanting to join a group and we had such a hard time with any groups letting us join, we decided to start our own," he says. "I think it's important to keep those doors open and give people that opportunity, so we seldom tell anyone who is interested no. If we say no, we might miss out on a good person who has something to contribute."

~~~~~

Strange Alaska and PEAK

Based out of Fairbanks, PEAK, which stands for Paranormal Explorers of Alaska, was started by friends Jessie Desmond and Ty Keltner. Originally called the UAF Paranormal Club, it evolved into a paranormal investigation club outside of the university. They re-established as a community group in August of 2008 and as of today, have roughly fourteen members. The team is made up a variety of paranormal enthusiasts, from a member who works for the FAA, to housewives, artists, and journalists.

Jessie has been conducting investigations for almost ten years. "I've always been interested in the paranormal and by cultural stories," she says. "I actually created my first paranormal group back in the fourth grade!"

Some of the places the group has investigated include Birch Hill Cemetery, the Open Market, a house next to Chapel of Chimes, and a private residence. Desmond states that the most interesting investigations so far have been the cemetery and the Open Market.

"I guess they were the most interesting because I went there not really expecting much of anything," she says, "but I walked away from both cases with multiple photos of orbs. The Chapel of Chimes house (right next to the funeral home) seemed to be a group favorite. We don't usually like to have a huge group of people there during investigations, but we made an exception for this one. I didn't really get much from that one, but other people did get some interesting photos."

Due to client privacy, Desmond is prohibited from disclosing some of her scarier experiences. "I can tell you though, I have had the sudden, overwhelming urge to leave a place when I was in the midst of taking some photos. I felt like someone was watching from the doorway. When I went back through my photos, there was an obvious orb in that same doorway."

PEAK is currently working towards getting a crypto investigation set up and trying to plan a trip to the Nenana area on a clear night to watch for UFO activity. Desmond says she has seen UFOs and has read up on the subject, but she has never done an actual investigation. "Due to our lack of experience, we are hoping to get the guys from SasquatchTracker.com to come guide us. I am more than ready for a Close Encounter!"

The group is also plans to publish a bi-annual magazine, *Strange Alaska*, with Alaskan-based paranormal, local legends, and other odd and interesting stories.

~~~~~

Sasquatch Trackers

M. Charlie Thompson came to Alaska in 1991, brought here by the Coast Guard and an interest that was originally sparked by reading Jack London's *The Call of the Wild* in 1975. Little did he know that his Alaskan adventures would include seeking out information and data on one of the wiliest of creatures—Sasquatch or, as Thompson likes to call it, "The Alaskan Yeti."

Thompson has been interested in Sasquatch for over thirty years, when he first heard stories about them back in 1977 while living in Idaho. In 2005, a report of a Sasquatch sighting along the Alaska Highway renewed his interest and he began actively researching and documenting incidents.

The team consists of two investigators, himself and associate Robert Alley. Alley, a Ketchikan resident, does his own research, but he and Thompson share reports of encounters and investigations. Thompson states that while he has never had anything happen that is truly unsettling, he has discovered tracks in two different locations and did have a strange feeling of being watched while in those locations.

"The tales of the Hairy Men are the same as Sasquatch," he says of the Alaskan folklore, "and I prefer the term Sasquatch or Yeti over Bigfoot. Bigfoot seems too Hollywood legend, while Sasquatch seems more like an existing animal."

He feels that Sasquatch is definitely an animal rather than any kind of human figure. "It's a primate," he says. "All the photos and videos I have seen over the years that show a profile or frame of Sasquatch's back do not show any evidence of a tail, so I think it is some kind of ape. Apes have what is called a sagittal crest, which gives them a cone-shaped head. Based on the evidence I have seen, Sasquatch has this cone-shaped head so it is not a humanoid in my opinion."

While Thompson has yet to have a real encounter with a Sasquatch, he continues to search and investigate the stories he hears.

A photo of what looks to be the footprint of an Alaskan Sasquatch.
Courtesy of M. Charlie Thompson, Sasquatch Trackers.

This shows just how huge these Sasquatch tracks really are!
Courtesy of M. Charlie Thompson, Sasquatch Trackers.

Afterword

While I still am not sure about the existence of ghosts, spirits, and paranormal activity, I find myself more on the side of believer than skeptic. Aside from the events told to me by some very believable, reasonable people, my belief boils down to something much simpler. I see life, despite the daily sadness and horror we see in the news, as a beautiful thing. People who tell me they wouldn't want to live past a certain age baffle me, for I have always seen each day as a gift, each birthday as a celebration—not something to be ignored, hidden, or lied about once we hit a certain milestone!

I wonder if those spirits or entities that remain in this world left behind children or other loved ones, and needed to be able to watch over them. Maybe there was unfinished business in their lives that they just couldn't let go of. Or maybe, like me, they simply loved life, grasping onto it with both hands, wringing every day dry, and being completely unwilling to depart.

I could see myself staying behind when I die. The thought of not knowing what happens next really bothers me. As a mother, the thought of my children going on with their lives without me is devastating, despite it being the natural order of things. In fact, it's kind of intriguing to consider that maybe someday (hopefully many years from now) it will be my spirit that people talk or write about, my image that will be seen in the reflection of a mirror, or my voice heard as a whisper in an empty room. I'd like to think that I have such a strong life force, something will remain.

In the end, we cannot know what will happen to us when we leave this world. So take every day as the gift it's intended to be, and leave your mark on the world so that if you cannot return from the next plane, you can be kept alive in the memories of those who loved you and whom you loved.

Index